THE
ARCHITECTURE
OF
VICTORIAN
LONDON

THE ARCHITECTURE OF VICTORIAN LONDON

John Summerson

UNIVERSITY PRESS
OF VIRGINIA
CHARLOTTESVILLE

Page-Barbour Lectures for 1972
University of Virginia

THE UNIVERSITY PRESS OF VIRGINIA
Copyright © 1976 by the Rector and Visitors
of the University of Virginia

First published 1976

Library of Congress Cataloging in Publication Data

Summerson, John Newenham, Sir, 1904–
    The architecture of Victorian London.

    1.   Architecture, Victorian—London.   2.   Archi-
tecture—London—History.   I.   Title.
NA970.S79   720′.9421   75–16130
ISBN 0–8139–0592–3

Printed in the United States of America

THE
ARCHITECTURE
OF
VICTORIAN
LONDON

1

The first thing I must say about my subject is that the spread of time across which it must necessarily run does not correspond with a tidy historical pattern. In this it is different from a related subject which I wrote about some years ago: Georgian London. The reigns of the four Georges coincided rather felicitously with the years during which the western part of London was actually put on the ground and also with a consistent development of classical taste from baroque, through Palladianism and rococo, to neoclassicism, which gave London the pictorial coherence which we can classify without too much distortion as "Georgian." The long reign of Victoria does not map out so happily. It begins just as the "Georgian" development of London is completing its course; it then enters a highly critical period of change—social, technological, architectural, culminating around 1870; after that, it goes on through years of elaboration and expansion till, crossing the twentieth century threshold, it leaves us with a state of affairs which we do not really want to call Victorian at all.

Nevertheless, the expression "Victorian London" is so firmly established and so much in use that I propose, in the present work, to accept the terms imposed by the lady monarch's regnal span and try to give you, in outline, an idea of what happened to London in its physical aspects between 1837 and 1901. I have three periods at my disposal and I propose to give a score of years to each, with liberty to stray across the twenty-year guidelines as convenience suggests. This, I think, is a safer plan than trying to discover "natural" junctures, which always become unnatural if you look at them too hard.

The very first thing to realize and remember about Victorian London is that the whole of its center and much of its perimeter was, in fact, Georgian. Victorian London *was* Georgian London and remained substantially Georgian till near the end of the century. It is only in our own time that the Georgian body has become fragmentary and residual. What "Victorian London" mostly means, therefore, is the imposition of new life-styles and their accompanying artifacts on an old fabric. It means the operations of the Victorian generations on the old map, both above and below the surface. It means the change of use of old buildings and the building of new. It means changes in structural method, scale, and style. It means the introduction not only of new buildings but of new types of building. At the end of it all it does not mean that we have anything like an integrated architectural whole. The old London which could be kept in the mind's eye as a comprehensibly historic organism had gone. The image of Victorian London is necessarily one of diversity and complexity and dispersal and even of disintegration.

As we enter the Victorian period there stands ahead of us a building so vast, so dominating, and of such sovereign importance that we must look at it respectfully before we pass on: I mean the Houses of Parliament (Fig. 1). It would be open to me to say that this is not a Victorian building. The old Palace of Westminster was burned down in 1834, and the competition for the new building was won by Charles Barry in 1835. So the design, at any rate, is pre-Victorian. But the construction, begun in 1840, continued through more than twenty years and was thus a Victorian performance from beginning to end. Nevertheless, the building does grow from Georgian roots, and I am sure that Horace Walpole would have loved it. The axial plan, turning on a central octagon, is an echo of Wyatt's Fonthill; the long, symmetrical, six-pavilioned river front was inspired by that classic performance so revered by the Palladians—Inigo Jones's design for Whitehall; the Gothic dress has the decorative intricacy which was what Georgians so admired about medieval architecture; the towers are placed as belvederes might be placed in a huge Italian villa. Not even the freshness of Pugin's invention in the details could warrant the building as a true child of the Victorian age.

Hence it is that sophisticated Victorians never really considered the Houses of Parliament as belonging to them. They either ignored or detested the building. Weale's comprehensive guide to London, celebrating the Exhibition year, 1851, devotes no less than eleven pages to destructive criticism. To Ruskin, in 1854, it was "the most effeminate and effectless heap of stones ever raised by man." If such criticism seems, today, excessively silly, it is worth considering why it was made. What upset Ruskin and others was not that the building had classical roots but that it was classical pretending to be Gothic and pretending in a specially

Fig. 1. The Palace of Westminster, designed by Charles
Barry in 1835 and substantially complete when he died
in 1860.

Fig. 2. The Reform Club, Pall Mall, 1836, where Barry proclaimed the Italian style that was to prevail in London till the seventies.

wicked way, by exploiting a kind of Gothic which was considered to be a low and corrupt version of the style. But there was perhaps more to it than that. Many early Victorians wanted to turn their backs on the age immediately preceding their own. To turn one's back on anything as big and expensive as the Houses of Parliament is a satisfying gesture, if not a very effective one.

The early Victorians could not, in fact, turn their backs on the Georgian age; they were caught in too many of its implications. They were rude about Sir Charles Barry's Gothic; but his Italian style, as exhibited in the Travellers' Club, the Reform Club (Fig. 2), and Bridgewater House, was the style more widely imitated than any other and which, for the first twenty-five years of the reign, was the characteristic language of nearly all new secular buildings.

Leaving the Houses of Parliament behind as a virtual nonparticipant in the Victorian story, let us take an ampler view of the mightily affluent and increasing metropolis of 1837. From the old central core, consisting of the ancient City and the Stuart and Georgian western outgrowth, London was moving fast, especially toward the northwest in Bayswater and to the southwest in Brompton. The mechanics of this movement were exactly those which had been moving London for a hundred years— estate development on the leasehold system. The northwestern and southwestern lands consisted of substantial acreages belonging to private families, bishoprics, charities, collegiate and other institutions. As the building tide approached, these landlords laid out streets and squares on their estates and let them off in plots or blocks of plots to builders. The builders, as they built houses on the plots, became entitled to leases (at a ground rent) of ninety-nine years. They then assigned the leases to the purchasers of the houses. The system was kept afloat by extensive mortgaging, this being a highly popular mode of investment for the middle classes. In responsible hands it was not a bad system. The whole of Regents Park and Regent Street had been developed by the Crown in that way, under the leadership of John Nash.

The system continued right through the Victorian period and was the means by which vast new middle-class quarters were created. They consisted of big houses, much bigger than the old Georgian types, with more spacious drawing rooms, better basements, and more bedrooms to accommodate the great servant population whose employment was the chief indulgence of the new rich. Architecturally, they inherited the forms and features of the age of Nash. The classical stuccoed terrace, the square with architectural elevations, the crescent—all these appear and reappear throughout the new areas. They make the "stucconia" in which the Veneerings of *Our Mutual Friend* had their super-affluent home. The architecture is more fulsome than Nash's, with a strong flavor of Charles Barry's Italian style. In the more affluent zones, the houses are better built.

From Tyburn (or Marble Arch, as we think of it since the arch got there in 1850) all the way to Shepherd's Bush—a matter of three and a quarter miles along the main highway leading west—are estates developed on these traditional lines in the thirties, forties, fifties, and sixties. The Bishop of London's estate on the east and the Ladbroke estate on the west are the biggest. The Bishop's estate started strongly in the Nash tradition with a few spectacular architectural performances, now mostly gone. In the forties came some novel enterprises like the parkway called Westbourne Terrace and the continuously bow-windowed Gloucester Terrace (Fig. 3), which we are hoping to preserve. On the Ladbroke estate is the striking layout called Stanley Gardens (Fig. 4), and on another smaller property are the twin Leinster and Princes squares, with the entrance porches facing each other across a central street and well-planted gardens shared between the houses behind each row. The planning of each estate allowed for the provision of *mews*—narrow cobbled streets flanked by stables, with coachmen's lodgings above, sometimes approached through a classical archway.

Not much is known, except their names, about the builders of these things or of their architects, who were rarely drawn from the upper ranks of the profession. The architecture is not at a high level. Collectively it produces an air of inert affluence, curiously at variance with the busy honeycomb of flats and bed-sitters which the houses have become—houses which in their prime were the well-groomed residences of lawyers, doctors, engineers, manufacturers, city men of all kinds, and of innumerable widows and spinsters, single ladies living at ease in a ten-room house with four or five servants and a rented pew in the nearest church.

Elsewhere in developing London of the forties and fifties the builders figure as more imposing characters. The area with the curious nickname of Pimlico, lying in a bulge of the Thames between Chelsea and Westminster, was developed almost entirely by one builder, Thomas Cubitt, who died in 1855. He was outstandingly the greatest builder of his period. He was the first to conduct a building business comprehending all the trades, working both as a contractor and as a developer and maintaining a "yard" which was on the lines of a well-organized factory. His main enterprises belong to the 1820s. The immensely solid stucco-fronted squares of Pimlico convey the dour competence of the Cubitt organization at its height. Cubitt, moreover, was the model for the next generation of London builders – those, for instance, who created the overwhelming monotony of the South Kensington area after 1852.

All these western and southwestern accretions to London are really the final phase of Georgian estate developments. They are urban, not suburban, and form part of the central mass of London buildings. They are all just within walking distance – and many Victorians, even rich ones, did walk – and easy omnibus rides, to the City. Beyond and behind them were more estates, more developments – areas of streets and squares less beneficially placed, inferior in quality, and descending in due course through the process of "lodging-house rot" to twilight wretchedness in our own time.

And there are the fringe developments with a true sub-urban self-consciousness. These are more interesting. Suburban estates were often projected with the sophisticated idea of a residential settlement of consistent and picturesque character, a character, however, invariably lost through lack of capital and the turn of the trade cycle. For the picturesque suburb, Nash had left a charming model in his Park Villages in Regents Park. These and a few illustrated books like Parker's *Villa Rustica* provided incentives to flights of fancy which, however, rarely got off the ground. Exceptionally ambitious was Henry E. Kendall's vision of Harlesden Park (Fig. 5). More typical of suburban estate development are the sober rows of semidetachment on the Eton Estate, Hampstead (Fig. 6).

If the early Victorians inherited and exploited the Georgian

Fig. 3. Gloucester Terrace, developed in the 1840s, a unique adaptation in Bayswater of the Georgian bow-window theme.

Fig. 4. Stanley Gardens, an Italian street composition of the 1850s on the Ladbroke estate, by Thomas Allom.

10

Fig. 5. Project (not executed) for an estate layout of 1845, Harlesden Park, by H. E. Kendall.

Fig. 6. Villa development of the 1840s and 1850s. Provost Road, on the estate of Eton College at Chalk Farm.

system of estate development, they also inherited, though hardly exploited, the policy of what was called "improvement." In John Nash's time "metropolitan improvements" was a term embracing enterprises of enormous scale—the development of Regents Park, the formation of Regent Street, the creation of Trafalgar Square, and a great deal else—in other words, the practice of what today we call town planning and urban renewal. All these enterprises were undertaken by the government under acts of Parliament enabling it to borrow money for the acquisition of property. A highly satisfactory return was ensured by the leasing of the sites along the newly created frontages. The government agency which looked after these things was called, perhaps rather oddly, the Office of Woods and Forests. When Regents Park and Regent Street were complete, this office was merged with two others, the Office of Land Revenue and the Office of Works and Buildings. The combined offices continued to promote the formation of new highways till 1851, when there was another reorganization. By that date they had formed several new streets, notably Cranbourn Street and New Oxford Street. There was no strict control of the architecture, as there had been in Nash's Regent Street, and the outcome was a not very edifying array of stylistic essays, including Greek, Italian, Louis XV, and even Elizabethan, by different architects.

The role of the central government in the development and adornment of the capital declined steeply after George IV. The mobilization of the Office of Woods and the Office of Works for anything beyond materialistic considerations had to be induced by public opinion, strongly led. It took a petition of 30,000 signatures to persuade the government to create a public park—Victoria Park—in the East End in 1842; and Battersea Park, five years later, was brought into being largely through pressure worked up by Thomas Cubitt and the local vicar. In Trafalgar Square a great opportunity was muddled away. The Nelson column (Fig. 7) was designed by a private architect who had won a government-sponsored competition. By the time the Office of Woods came to consider a layout for the square, with Sir Charles Barry's advice, the government was committed, and the monster—"our great national eye-sore," as the *Times* called it—had to be built and the scale and character of the square destroyed.

Fig. 7. Trafalgar Square, about 1900, showing Barry's
layout and the Nelson column of 1839–42, designed by
William Railton.

13

Fig. 8. The Public Record Office, Chancery Lane,
designed by James Pennethorne, 1851–66; one of the
few Gothic public buildings of its time.

Fig. 9. Edward Blore's new front for Buckingham Palace. Built in 1841–47, it was replaced by the present front in 1913.

Fig. 10. The Royal Exchange, the central secular monument of the City of London; designed by William Tite, 1842–44, after its predecessor had been destroyed by fire.

Public buildings had necessarily to be undertaken from time to time, and if they were of any size or importance the designs were obtained in competition, on the precedent of the Houses of Parliament. There was indeed one government architect of great distinction—Sir James Pennethorne. He was used as a sort of advisory dogsbody both for the street improvements of the Office of Woods and the new buildings of the Office of Works. Both Victoria Park and Battersea Park owe their scenic character to him. Of the few buildings he was actually allowed to design and build, the Public Record Office in Chancery Lane (Fig. 8), the only Gothic public building after the Houses of Parliament, and the building in Burlington Gardens, designed to house the nascent London University, are the best-known survivors.

The most prominent public building after the Houses of Parliament was the new block built across the east front of Buckingham Palace in 1841–47 (Fig. 9). It was designed by Edward Blore to cover up what was generally regarded as a disgraceful performance by Nash and to present a conventionally decent front to the Mall. Nobody ever thought much of it and it was replaced in 1913. Its mediocrity typifies the general disinclination, outside as well as inside Parliament, to spend either money or talent on public works. Victorian London was in this respect the very antithesis of Napoleon III's Paris. Never was there anything which could be called a public works program. London was a metropolis which grew by the initiative of landlords and builders, by competitive pressures in business, by religious or humanitarian philanthropy, and, in an almost negligible measure, by the action of the central government.

This however was not quite true of that part of London called the City. The City was to a great extent self-governing, with its medieval guild organization culminating in the authority of the lord mayor, aldermen, and Common Council. The City looked after its own "improvements" and regarded with a jealous and often hostile eye whatever went on outside its boundaries. In 1837 the City had just completed some very important improvements, and as these were to set the scene for the greatest rebuilding of the City since 1666 they are worth attention.

London Bridge, seven centuries old and in part rebuilt, having at last failed, a new bridge designed by John Rennie was opened by William IV in 1831. Leading northwest from the new bridge, a new street, King William Street, was cut, leading to a point where four ancient streets converged–Cheapside, Threadneedle Street, Cornhill, and Lombard Street. This point was the long-accepted "center" of the City. Here the Mansion House (the lord mayor's residence) looked across to the Bank of England, while a little way up Cornhill was the time-honored focus of London's mercantile life, the Royal Exchange. In January 1838, six months after Victoria's accession, the Royal Exchange was burned to the ground. It was the most sensational burning since that of the Houses of Parliament, four years earlier. It was also, from the point of view of improvement, a great stroke of luck. With the acquisition and demolition of a piece of property westward of the old building, it was possible to reorientate the Royal Exchange and give the new building a facade looking west across open space toward Cheapside. With the Mansion House to the south and the Bank of England to the north–both distinguished classical buildings–the space took on something of the aspect of a forum, an aspect which it still, in spite of much rebuilding and a maelstrom of traffic, retains.

The design for the new Royal Exchange, built in 1842–44, was the product of a disgracefully mismanaged competition won by a young architect with friends in the City–William Tite. Its main exterior feature is a huge Corinthian portico (Fig. 10). Behind this is a *cortile* modeled on that of the Farnese Palace and built there for the simple reason that the Royal Exchange had done business in an open court ever since Elizabeth I; only in 1880 was it covered over with iron and glass. The building is of noble scale, but perhaps only moderate architectural interest, and is now totally useless; but as a monument it registers the beginning of a great phase in the City's history–the mid-Victorian rebuilding which, by accident, it inaugurated.

The rebuilding of the City in the course of its transformation from a mixed business and residential quarter to an exclusively countinghouse area of fabulous site values is one of the most dramatic aspects of Victorian London and will engage our attention at various times. This is the place to say something of its beginnings.

The main bidders for conspicuous sites in the City of the thirties and forties were joint-stock banks and assurance companies, and of the two it was the assurance companies which were the more competitive and the more ambitious to make an architectural hit. Banking was an essentially conservative area of English life, bound up with family traditions and aristocratic and political relationships. The private banker was a man of peculiar esteem. His bank was also his residence, barely differentiated from any other rich man's residence. The coming of the joint-stock bank, a business sheltering under corporate anonymity, was a shock to this traditional system. But the shock was soon absorbed, and the joint-stock establishments quickly earned the trust and esteem awarded to the private houses. One of the first joint-stock banks to be accepted was the London and Westminster (Fig. 11). Founded in 1833, it built itself new premises in Lothbury, opposite the north front of the Bank of England, in 1839, the directors employing the Bank of England architect, C. R. Cockerell (he had succeeded Soane there in 1833), for the facade. The building was unmistakably an official, not a domestic, building, the first bank apart from the Bank of England to look like a bank, with allegories of London and Westminster above the cornice. The private bankers did not attempt to compete with this until, in 1858, the largest of them, Jones Loyd, actually built new premises next door. These, appropriately, had all the appearance of a private mansion. But the show of independence was an empty one. The merging of Jones Loyd with the London and Westminster was one of the sensations of 1864.

But it was the assurance companies, with their less mature and gentlemanly background, which contributed most to the monumentalization of City architecture. Assurance companies needed to create a public image of affluence and security. To build in the style of a public building was—as it still is—one way of doing this. Such buildings first appeared in the West End, the Strand, and Fleet Street; but in 1838 the Globe, a company which fourteen years earlier had successfully broken the monopoly of the chartered companies, seized one of the finest sites in the City, where Cornhill and Lombard Street converge (Fig. 12). The company employed Philip Hardwick; his building was pleasant enough, but here it was site that mattered. Simultaneously, the Marine came to Cornhill with a facade sculpturally enriched with figures of Navigation and Hope. In 1839, Thomas Hopper's Atlas building, inspired by Inigo Jones and with a striking representation of Atlas over the door, arrived in Cheapside. In 1840, with the widening of Bartholomew Lane, new sites became available opposite the Bank of England. The Alliance installed itself here, while to the corner of the Lane and Threadneedle Street came the Sun, with a building of the highest distinction designed by Cockerell and demolished only in 1971. In Lothbury, again opposite the Bank, the Alfred Life office was built in 1843; and the Imperial office at the corner of Threadneedle and Old Broad streets in 1848.

But these were only beginnings. The rage for assurance promotion after 1844 was such that by 1851 there were 125 assurance companies in London, 32 of which were less than seven years old. Competition was intense, and the companies that prevailed invariably felt the obligation to lodge themselves conspicuously in the City. The Royal Exchange area was the great magnet. In 1856–58, the County Fire and Provident Life, the Colonial Life, and the supremely successful Royal all housed themselves magnificently in Lombard Street, hitherto almost sacred to private banking. Eighteen fifty-eight was the culminating year. Twelve companies, in rapid succession, failed, and the assurance mania was over. The survivors, however, blossomed as never before, and assurance expansion was a considerable factor in the architecture of Victorian London.

The style of these buildings was invariably Italian, with something of the comfortable monumentality but none of the reserve of Barry's Pall Mall clubs. Allegorical sculpture was liberally distributed. After 1858 there were some divergent stylistic departures, and to these I shall come later. Meanwhile it must be said that banks and assurance companies, though the showiest, were not the only agents in the great rebuilding. Warehouses and countinghouses for manufacturers and importers played their part. The extension of Cannon Street into St. Paul's Churchyard provided sites for many, including one monster warehouse for Cook, the wholesale draper, which kept the sunlight off Wren's masterpiece for three generations. It was felt at the time that Manchester architects ordered these things better. Another type of building which developed in the forties and fifties was the

Fig. 11. Philip Charles Hardwick's design for the Jones
Loyd banking house, Lothbury, 1858. To the right is
C. R. Cockerell's London and Westminster Bank of 1839.

Fig. 12. The City scene in 1838, showing (left of center)
the Globe Insurance building, by Philip Hardwick.

block of "chambers" intended for lettable office accommodation. A building designed solely for this purpose was built as early as 1825. Twenty years later came a large and important specimen next to the Royal Exchange, and what today we call the "office block" had made its appearance. Assurance companies and credit houses saw here an opportunity of combining prestige with investment. A mighty Italian facade, on a prestigious site, could cover, besides a handsome business area and boardroom, several floors of revenue-producing space.

So far, all the buildings we have noticed may be seen as quite natural derivatives or modified versions of Georgian types. We have seen nothing at all revolutionary. No decisively new types have emerged. The trend in style from quasi-Greek simplicity to Italian ornateness has been intensified, and there is a new bigness of scale. I have said nothing much yet of churches and so nothing of Gothic, for the intrusion of Gothic into secular urban architecture had scarcely begun, notwithstanding the Houses of Parliament. To churches I shall come later. It is time now to consider those things which emerge in London of the forties and fifties as absolutely new, the disturbing things which show that we are on the eve of profound change. The joint products of steam and iron are only some of these but they are among the most important, and we may start with the coming of railways and their accompanying buildings.

The first group of railways came to London between 1836 and 1857. They did not enter the capital but came all the way through open fields and stopped at points where the main centers were readily accessible. There they built the first terminal stations. These early stations consisted of two parts—the shed covering the tracks and the front building containing waiting rooms and offices. In the earliest stations the shed was an empirical construction of little interest, while the front building was architecture. The famous portico at Euston (1835–40), lost through the fumbling evasions of administrators, was not even a front building in this sense; it was an architectural approach to the railway company's land in an entirely Georgian idiom and on the axis of an existing Georgian square. At Nine Elms (1837–38) the shed was negligible and the front building was a version of the functionalist classicism of J. N. L. Durand. At London Bridge (1844) the front building was rather like a country villa in the style of Sir Charles Barry; at Bricklayers Arms (1844) it was a picturesque arched screen with quaint Italian details; in neither case was the shed more advanced than the kind of structure that might have been built years earlier to shelter carts or merchandise. Then, in 1851, came King's Cross, the only one of the series still standing (Fig. 13). Here the booking offices and waiting rooms are at the side, and the sheds themselves are the expressive parts. They consist of a majestic pair of naves separated by a brick arcade and closed on the town side by a massive brick screen in the Durand style. The naves are arched over with ribs that were of laminated timber later replaced by iron.

With King's Cross the railway station reached architectural self-consciousness. The next great terminal was Paddington (1852–54) (Fig. 14), still more self-conscious and designed in the new spirit of artistic adventure which hovered round that exciting year 1851. For at Paddington, Brunel, the engineer, and Digby Wyatt, the artistic adviser, tried to invent an architecture for iron with a style of its own. It was a style compounded of many styles —an attempt to advance artistically from the more strictly functional building which had posed the problem of iron and art so very conspicuously—the Crystal Palace.

The Crystal Palace (Fig. 15) was a wholly unique temporary structure built in Hyde Park for a particular occasion. By a stupendous feat of industrial organization it was conceived and built in nine months. It was opened by the Queen on 1 May 1851 and it closed its doors six months later. But that was not the end. The palace itself was moved to a hilltop site at Sydenham, where, in a greatly enlarged form, it lasted till 1937. More important, the palace, as well as its contents and the whole occasion of its building, served to focus the doubts and discontents about the architecture of the period and to raise in an acute form the question already being debated by young architects: What was to be the architectural style of the Victorian age?

If we look carefully around London of the forties and fifties we can find some of the tentative answers. We find them in a variety of places—here in a church, there in a school, a public hall, a warehouse. Thus, in 1840, in the remote southern suburb of Streatham Hill, a cheap brick church was built to the design of an unknown young architect, James Wild (Fig. 16). He had been an archaeologist with Lepsius in Egypt and had seen something of the Near East. He had also, evidently, seen the published works of Schinkel, whence comes, perhaps, some of the force of his composition. He was also brother-in-law of a more famous designer, Owen Jones. Owen Jones, like Wild, had experience of Near Eastern and Islamic art, and had compiled a marvelous monograph on the Alhambra. He was artistic supervisor of the Crystal Palace, where he decided the color scheme. His own architecture included St. James's Hall, Piccadilly, 1857–58 (Fig. 17). There he tried to improvise a new style for a new occasion, much as Digby Wyatt had tried to do at Paddington. Another pointer to new ways was a humble school off Endell Street built by Wild in a version of Venetian Gothic in 1844, five years before Ruskin drew attention to the style. In the City, J. B. Bunning, the City architect, built in 1846–49 the Coal Exchange, with a domed hall (Fig. 18), all in decorative cast and wrought iron. The reading room of the British Museum, formed in 1845–47 by covering a courtyard with a huge iron dome, was another impressive adventure, while here and there among the City warehouses were experiments with new shapes and patterned bricks.

These movements toward some kind of "modernism" never came to much, though their effect can be traced through the sixties and beyond. The movement which rose to real power in the forties and fifties was, of course, the Gothic revival. This, however, was mainly associated with churches and with the Anglican revival of ritual. Church-building was one of the most significant and visually conspicuous elements in early Victorian London. Through the first twenty years of the reign, about six new churches were built every year. The motives for building and the character of the results are important.

Before 1837 nearly all church-building throughout England was assisted, sometimes very substantially, by the state, less out of piety than a feeling that social stability was in part dependent on religious orthodoxy. The reforms of the thirties greatly reduced this incentive. Moreover, churchmen of the new school were beginning to feel that the state was not the proper agency for church-building. People should build their own churches as they had done in the good old days. Thus, in 1836, the "church

Fig. 13. King's Cross Station, designed by Lewis Cubitt
in 1851. The brick front expresses the two timber-arched
sheds behind.

Fig. 14. Paddington Station, 1852–54, designed in iron by
Isambard Kingdom Brunel, with the artistic collaboration
of Matthew Digby Wyatt.

Fig. 15. The main avenue of the Crystal Palace, 1851. Designed by Joseph Paxton, it was rebuilt in an enlarged form at Sydenham in 1852 and burned down in 1937.

Fig. 16. Christ Church, Streatham Hill, designed by
James Wild, 1840.

Fig. 17. St. James's Hall, Piccadilly, 1857–58 (demolished
1905), where Owen Jones attempted to create a new
style for a modern type of building.

Fig. 18. The Coal Exchange, an artistic enterprise in iron
construction and decorative design by the City architect,
J. B. Bunning, 1846–49 (demolished).

extension" movement was inaugurated. The chief instigator was Bishop Blomfield of London, and his Metropolis Churches Fund aimed at raising money for fifty new churches. It was followed by local funds to build churches in outlying areas of suburban London. When Blomfield resigned in 1856, he had consecrated some 200 churches in his diocese, most of them in London itself.

The incentives toward church-building were, of course, not all of one kind nor all entirely religious in inspiration. The presence of a church, or the prospect of one, was an essential element in successful estate development. Any prudent landowner, in laying out his property for building, would earmark a central and shapely piece of ground for a church and be prepared, moreover, to make a gift of £500 or so toward its building. The church would stamp the estate with a good middle-class character; no radicalism, no nonconformity. The actual promotion of the build-ing would be in the hands of a local committee. They would solicit subscriptions in the area, and apply to the bishop's fund or any local fund there might be, and also to the Incorporated Church-building Society, for grants. And so the church would rise. It would be served from the mother church of the parish until the district was formed into a parish endowed by the ec-clesiastical commissioners with a vicar of its own. Often the first vicar of such a parish would be a young curate who had exerted himself in the formation of the committee and the raising of funds.

This is the pattern of church-building throughout suburban London in the early Victorian years. Outside this pattern are a smaller number of churches built by rich patrons with a view to bringing the consolation of high churchmanship and beautiful architecture to some of the duskier quarters of London. These churches are often more important, architecturally, than the es-tate churches. The rich patron tended to employ an architect who shared his ideas and ideals, while the average landowner would probably wish to commit the church on his land to the ar-chitect, of whatever sort, who had laid out the estate.

Nearly all the churches we are concerned with here are Gothic. A few are Romanesque and one, and one only, is Renaissance Italian. They embody the early progress of the Gothic revival, from the painfully feeble efforts of late Georgian architects, working with exiguous grants from the parliamentary commissioners, to the highly competent imitations of thirteenth- or fourteenth-century churches of which a fair number of architects were capable by the late fifties. The influence of Pugin, through his buildings and writings, is strong, though as it happens he built little in London—only the Roman Catholic Cathedral of St. George, Southwark, begun in 1840, and a small Catholic church in Fulham.

A pioneer in the building of these "correct" Gothic churches in London was George Gilbert Scott, who rebuilt the burned parish church of St. Giles at Camberwell on scholarly fourteenth-century lines in 1840. In 1847 Benjamin Ferrey, Pugin's friend and biographer, built for the philanthropic millionairess Baroness Burdett-Coutts a rich little fourteenth-century church in the twilight area of Rochester Row (Fig. 19); and in the same year came St. Barnabas, Pimlico, by Thomas Cundy, assisted by William Butterfield, a church built for the Pimlico poor with funds extracted from the Belgravian rich by an eloquent vicar. To 1849–52, in contrast, belongs St. Mary Magdalen, Munster Square, a model fourteenth-century church by R. C. Carpenter, built through the efforts of a clergyman dedicated to the service of the poor. Also to 1849 belong the beginnings of the most striking church of the period—All Saints, Margaret Street (Fig. 20), built by William Butterfield for a committee of High Church devotees. All Saints was the first church to break away from the revival's dogmatic addiction to English fourteenth-century models. In composition, in proportion, in material, and in detail it was eclectic and original. Massed round a tiny courtyard, with a narrow foreign-looking steeple leaping up from one corner, its black-striped red brickwork challenged all accepted ideas of what Gothic revivalism was supposed to be. Wild's church at Streatham had been original but it was, stylistically, outside the revival. All Saints was by one of the revival's acknowledged leaders; it let loose a cataract of innovations.

Scott, Carpenter, and Butterfield were the leaders of the revival in the Anglican church, and their subsequent fame underlines the esteem of church-building at this period. To those names should be added that of J. L. Pearson, whose Holy Trinity, Bessborough Gardens, of 1849, built at the expense of a rich and well-

Fig. 19. St. Stephen, Rochester Row, Westminster, by
Benjamin Ferrey; an example of the "middle-pointed" style
in a London church of 1847.

Fig. 20. All Saints, Margaret Street; William Butterfield's famous innovative church of 1849.

connected archdeacon, was perhaps the most perfect specimen of the orthodox school of scholarly imitators. All four of these architects contributed much to Victorian London, and not only in church-building. But it was in church-building that they made their names and achieved lasting fame. The architects of London's banks and office buildings, warehouses, hotels, and public halls, the creators of estate plans, and the designers of streets had no such success. Nor did Gothic revival practice penetrate very far into the general mass of London building work. In studying the architecture of Victorian London as a whole, the participation of the Gothic movement must be understood in a correct perspective and not awarded undue prominence.

Our survey of London in the first two decades of Victoria's reign must conclude with a diversion from architecture toward a subject of radical importance for the whole future of the capital, namely, its administration. In 1835, the Municipal Corporation Act had been passed. This gave to every major center of population in Britain except one a basis of democratic self-government—and the exception was London. The reasons for London's exclusion are complex; one of them was the self-sufficiency and jealousy of the City in pursuing what it conceived to be its own interests. By 1851 there was the extraordinary situation of a metropolis of 2,300,000 persons of whom only 130,000 in one small area of the whole enjoyed the advantages of corporate government. Outside the City, such control as there was issued from a chaos of boards—paving, lighting, cleansing, and others—each originating in a local act of Parliament. There were some 300 of these boards, mostly self-elected and acting with sublime indifference to each other. There was almost no control of buildings in the fringe areas until the Metropolitan Buildings Act of 1844, and this was incompetently administered. As to sewers, in seven years the various bodies of commissioners that had been brought into one commission in 1848 had succeeded in building, at huge expense, one sewer.

The incidence of cholera, the stink of the Thames, and the filth of the outer suburbs at length roused Parliament to action, and a bill brought in by Sir Benjamin Hall received the royal assent in 1855. This was not by any means a measure to provide local government for London but simply one to erect a competent elected body with powers to deal comprehensively with the major physical horrors of the capital. The body thus created was the Metropolitan Board of Works, elected through twenty-three parochial vestries and thirteen districts made up of smaller vestries. To the vestries and districts were assigned the functions of the old paving, lighting, and cleansing boards. The Metropolitan Board itself was to be responsible for two main issues. First, it was to secure the complete liberation of the Thames from the sewage of the capital. Second, it was to establish better communications in London by widening streets and creating new ones. These two issues, separately and in combination, had, over the next twenty years, an incalculable effect on the whole physical character of London. How these effects worked out and what kind of architectural scenery it was in which they resulted will be my next concern.

2

I have already mentioned the Metropolitan Board of Works, the body created by Parliament in 1855 to do two things, principally, for London: first, to give it an efficient drainage system; second, to make new highways. The main drainage—the liberation of London from the curse of its own sewage—was a tremendous structural undertaking but one which, being mostly out of sight, hardly comes within the purview of these discourses. Nevertheless, it did have one most pronounced effect on visible London because it precipitated the construction of the Thames embankments. These had long been desired both as the bearers of riverside highways and for the convenience and safety of shipping. But it was the sewage plan which made at least the northern embankment an absolute necessity. Sir Joseph Bazalgette, the MBW's engineer, solved the sewage problem with masterly simplicity. All the old sewers of London flowed (diagrammatically speaking) north-south or south-north into the Thames. Some had been natural rivers and streams. Bazalgette's plan was to construct a series of huge brick sewers intercepting all of them and flowing from west to east through London and then onward to outfalls in the estuary. There were to be three intercepting sewers north of the river and two on the south. On the north, to construct the high- and mid-level sewers was relatively easy; the low-level sewer was far more difficult. To lay it under or near the Strand or Fleet Street offered a vista of destruction and disruption too hideous to contemplate. The only place for the low-level sewer was on the river bank itself, and to put it there meant the construction of an embankment. Hence the Victoria Embankment, running from the Houses of Parliament to Blackfriars, begun in 1862 and opened in 1870. On the south bank there was not the same problem, but there *was* a perennial problem of flooding. Hence the Albert Embankment, running west from Westminster Bridge to Vauxhall (Fig. 21).

These embankments modified the London image in two ways. First, their projection into the river had the effect of "shelving" existing buildings facing the river. Thus the magnificent Somerset House, built by Chambers in 1775–80 with its own arched embankment and water gates, became entirely isolated from the water, losing much of its dignity; so did the Adams' Adelphi. Second, the creation of the embankments put an entirely new value on riverside properties and invited redevelopment on a great scale. Hotels and institutions eventually filled up the spaces on the north. On the south, opposite the Houses of Parliament, came St. Thomas's Hospital, London's first modern hospital.

The embankments themselves are noble granite walls with few architectural trimmings. Such as there are were the work of the MBW's architect, George Vulliamy, who had been a clerk under Barry. His are the famous embankment lamps with the entwined dolphins; also the architectural setting of "Cleopatra's Needle," Mehemet Ali's somewhat unwieldy gift to the British government set up in 1877. Behind the granite walls are tunnels for gas and water mains. Behind these is the low-level intercepting sewer. Behind this again is the cut-and-cover tunnel of the District Railway, which arrived, as we shall see, just in time to be included in the embankment package.

The embankments were a triumph for the MBW. The buildings that line them came mostly after 1877, and some we shall come to later. For the present we must go back a few years and consider the map of "improvement" to which London of the fifties and sixties was subjected—in particular, Victoria Street. Victoria Street is a highway running west-southwest from Westminster Abbey, through a tangle of ancient streets, to the smart new developments in Belgravia. It was promoted neither by the Office of Woods and Forests nor by the Metropolitan Board of Works, but by commissioners empowered under an act of 1845 to raise up to £250,000 and to lend money to builders. After some imprudent management had been straightened out by further acts, the street was opened in 1851. It filled up slowly and was not fully built till 1895.

Victoria Street is typical of the crude surgery of early Victorian urbanists. It forced its way across the map quite regardless of lateral relationships. Even today, after so much rebuilding, Victoria Street is a bleak corridor a mile and a quarter long out of which you turn, if you must, left or right, into a labyrinthine perpetuation of sixteenth- and seventeenth-century development —without, of course, the sixteenth- and seventeenth-century buildings.

Fig. 21. The Thames embankments, seen from the terrace of County Hall, with Charing Cross railway bridge and (far left) Whitehall Court.

The interesting thing about Victoria Street is that the line it took through the old labyrinth had the effect of creating new frontages of exceptional length, if not of any great depth. When these new frontages were placed on the market they offered a challenge to new types of investment. Some of them, at the near and far ends of the street, were taken up quite soon with important results. To Victoria Street came the first blocks of middle-class flats in London, the first monster hotel, and the first West End block of offices. The flats were pulled down in 1971, the offices some twenty years earlier. The hotel, now offices, has been altered out of recognition.

The flats, at the west end of the street, were built by a developer named Mackenzie, a Scotsman, and designed by Henry Ashton. They were described on completion in 1853 as supplying "what has long been a desideratum in London, namely, complete residences on flats, as in Edinburgh and Paris" (*flats*, meaning "apartments," comes from Scotland). The novelty for London was that they were "complete residences" and not mere "chambers" such as bachelors were accustomed to in Albany or lawyers in the Inns of Court; nor were they utilitarian like the "model dwellings" which philanthropists were promoting for the working class. They were meant for respectable families who only required to spend part of the year in London and were offered at rents between £80 and £200 a year. They do not seem to have let very well, nor were they soon imitated. However, it was in and about Victoria Street that the flat principle eventually took root.

The hotel, called the Westminster Palace Hotel (Fig. 22), was built at the east end of the street, nearly opposite Westminster Abbey, in 1857–61. It followed, but completely eclipsed, the Great Western Railway's hotel at Paddington, then just finished, and was the first to be described as a "monster" hotel. It had 286 rooms (bedrooms and sitting rooms), 70 WCs, and 14 bathrooms, a vast coffee room, and an even vaster banqueting room; an "ascending carriage" (in other words a lift, the first passenger lift in London) that worked on Sir William Armstrong's hydraulic principle; a pneumatic bell system with seven miles of pipes and 400 bells; and hoists and speaking tubes everywhere. The Westminster Palace brought England abreast of France and America

Fig. 22. Westminster Palace Hotel, built in 1857–61. It is now an office building and has been "de-Victorianized."

in the international hotel scramble. With its favorable position opposite the Houses of Parliament, where the law courts were still centered, it was an immediate success and remained one of the leading hotels until the coming of even more fabulous monsters like the Savoy and the Cecil on the Victoria Embankment.

The office block, called Westminster Chambers, built in 1861–63, stood opposite to the hotel. Buildings devoted entirely to lettable offices were appearing in the City, and this was the first of any size in the West. The developers were the Mutual Tontine Association, who issued ordinary shares as well as inviting subscriptions on the tontine principle. The frontage was immensely long, so the building was divided into seven sections, each with fourteen sets of chambers and four or five rooms in each set. The idea was that the chambers would be taken by parliamentary solicitors and agents and professional men in general; in fact, it became the almost exclusive resort of civil engineers.

To Victoria Street, along with flats, hotel, and offices, came a rather unexpected enterprise—a huge whiskey distillery in early Gothic. The building partly survives as one of London's best-known multiple stores—the Army and Navy.

These four examples show how the formation of a new street attracted the investment of capital in new types of building; the increasing size of sites offering, especially in the case of the hotel, the opportunity to benefit by economies of scale which could not be exercised in ordinary London rebuildings. As to the architectural results, they are certainly poor, as usually happens when the economic and functional stakes are high. Ashton's flats had decent, if rather overwindowed, street fronts with some Palladian decorations and arches to accommodate the shops. The architect of the hotel, Andrew Mosely, said in a lecture that he hoped his building "would possess at least some indication of 'high art,' untrammelled by conventionalities," but nobody was enthusiastic. The office block was more or less in Barry's style, which, as it was designed by Barry's former chief clerk in partnership with Barry's son Charles, is what one would expect. But the genius of Sir Charles had not been transmitted.

Four years after Victoria Street was opened the whole business of London "improvements," which included the cutting of new highways, became vested in the Metropolitan Board of Works.

We have seen how and why the board came into being in 1855, and what it so splendidly achieved in the installation of the main drainage and the construction of the embankments. In its function of street-making, apart from the embankment, its performance was less glorious. Compared with Haussmann's exactly contemporary planning dictatorship in Paris, it lacked powers, energy, and vision. Never at any time did it take as broad a view of London's problems as Nash or his successor Pennethorne had done. It was, in effect, a mere agency for the submission of projects to Parliament and the supervision of their subsequent execution. The board rarely, if ever, proposed improvements. It received deputations from the vestries and district boards, considered their proposals, arranged priorities, initiated legislation, and, in due course, put the finalized plans into effect and sold or leased the surplus land. Its control of architecture was negligible.

Nevertheless, the sum total of the MBW's operations is not unimpressive. In the course of the thirty-four years of its existence it carried out forty-two improvements at a total net cost (the sales of surplus land being deducted) of nearly £7,500,000. This does not include the Thames embankments, which cost nearly £2,500,000. In other words £10,000,000 was spent in the course of a generation on the making of new highways which, in nearly every case, created new building sites, new building enterprises, and new architecture.

The board's first two undertakings were Garrick Street and Southwark Street. Garrick Street was a much-needed outlet from the busy Covent Garden market into St. Martin's Lane—a short street where the surplus land produced some oddly shaped sites behind the new frontages. The first arrival was the Garrick Club, with a front in a gloomy version of Barry's Pall Mall style: the club gave the street its name. Then came the prestige premises of a firm of auctioneers (Fig. 23) with, next door, the elegantly detailed Italian offices of the Westminster Insurance Company. Finally, in 1864, came the premises of a stained glass manufacturer, Lavers and Barraud, wedged in a highly awkward and presumably cheap corner site and designed by a young architect, A. W. Blomfield, in the fashionably severe Gothic of the moment. Garrick Street survives intact, even with some of the shopfronts. It is a nice example of the way things were done in the

Fig. 23. Premises of a well-known firm of auctioneers in Garrick Street, developed 1855–64. The architect was Thomas Allom.

Fig. 24. Part of the Grosvenor Hotel, Victoria Station, built in 1860–61.

sixties: a road slashed through an old quarter, sites behind the new frontages shaped more or less by the accidents of property acquisition, then a laissez-faire policy as to who took the sites and what sort of buildings they built.

Southwark Street was a rather different affair—a longish street (two-thirds of a mile) in a part of South London largely dedicated to warehousing and to the hop trade in particular. Special need for the street, long envisaged, arose from the development of traffic at London Bridge Station. When the eastern half was finished in 1862, the warehouses began to arrive and the street to take on a character unlike any other in London. The new types of warehouse were daringly architectural—sometimes Venetian or French Romanesque, sometimes early Gothic, sometimes in the palazzo style, and nearly always with nice, gay polychromy in colored brick and stone. The palazzo style prevailed sufficiently for a contemporary to draw a parallel with Pall Mall and the clubs.

After Southwark Street the MBW occupied itself with a street opening up parts of the East End of London and then, from 1862, with the most majestic of its undertakings, the Victoria Embankment, of which enough has already been said. One of the several purposes of the embankment was to create a highway which should draw off east-west traffic from the City and ease congestion in Cheapside, Ludgate Hill, Fleet Street, and the Strand. This necessarily required an extension from the east end of the embankment to the City center at the Bank and the Mansion House—a new street right through the old City. This was proposed by the MBW and, after some sparring with the City Fathers, who did not care to have such brash and immature promoters operating within their boundaries, the necessary act was passed in 1863. And so a street was made and called, with due loyalty but singular lack of invention, Queen Victoria Street. It was mostly built up in the late sixties and early seventies, and to some of its architecture we shall come later.

At the west end of the new embankment there was a similar need for a connecting highway to bring the traffic out at Charing Cross. Northumberland House, the last of London's riverside palaces, stood in the way; but the Duke of Northumberland, being persuaded that the demolition of his home was a matter of public necessity, consented to dispose of it for £500,000 and Northumberland Avenue was formed. It became a street of monster hotels and monster clubs, the architecture of which belongs to the eighties.

The forming of new highways is only one aspect of the veritable fury of constructional alteration which London underwent in the course of the 1860s. The other most significant aspect is the new onset of railway construction. Previously I mentioned the early terminal stations as being situated on what were then the fringes of the capital. They represented the first stage only of the railway assault. The second stage came with the struggle by the southern companies to get their trains across the Thames and into central London. Between the two stages something else started—the underground. Between 1860 and 1863 London saw the building of the first underground railway in the world—the Metropolitan Railway. It ran, mostly in cut-and-cover tunnels under the streets, from Paddington to King's Cross and on to Farringdon Street. Thousands of passengers still travel daily under John Fowler's low-sprung elliptical arches. Later came the District Railway, which, as we have seen, got itself inside the embankment. Between them the two companies eventually threw round central London the underground belt called the Inner Circle, a main element in London's underground system.

The underground, naturally, produced little above the surface except small cement-faced kiosks containing ticket offices—sad little buildings, some hopefully domed for effect. With the main-line railways it was a different matter. These did have a large impact on the London scene. They built viaducts across the streets, bridges over the Thames, terminal station sheds in central areas, and, most conspicuous of all, station hotels.

The first southern line to cross the Thames was the London Brighton and South Coast Railway, though it was actually an associate company which built the Pimlico bridge (1859–60) and Victoria Station (1862), the new station strategically situated at the west end of the new Victoria Street. Actually, two stations were built on the site—one for the LB & SCR and another, next door, for the London, Chatham and Dover. The story is a complicated one, and Victoria Station is, as a result, London's most confusing terminal. The two station sheds, separated by an arched brick wall, have different types of iron construction, and originally there was not much else but the sheds—except, indeed, the hotel.

The Grosvenor Hotel, at Victoria (Fig. 24), built by a subsidiary company in 1860–61, was seen at once as a portent: "one of those striking conceptions which distinctively mark the civilization of the age." The architect was J. T. Knowles, a man whose career in architecture merged with an even more striking career in political journalism—he founded *The Nineteenth Century* magazine. The Grosvenor magnificently typifies its period. In its massive uniformity it inherits something from Barry's school; in the naturalistic whimsicality of its detail it echoes Ruskin; in its deliberate coarseness it speaks for the age of steam. Still much as it has always been, it is one of the representative monuments of Victorian London.

In 1864–66 two more railways crossed the Thames; three more bridges were built and three more terminals established on the north bank, two of them with hotels. There was an epic struggle between the South Eastern Railway Company and the London, Chatham and Dover. The secretary of the South Eastern was no less a figure than Samuel Smiles, of *Self Help* fame. Under his intrepid leadership, the South Eastern secured the site of a decaying market at Charing Cross. Its southern terminal was at London Bridge, two miles away. To bring trains from London Bridge to Charing Cross required seventeen bridges, 190 brick arches, and an iron viaduct over Southwark Market, the buying out of old St. Thomas's Hospital, the demolition of almshouses, the removal of 8,000 bodies from a graveyard, the dismantling of Hungerford suspension bridge, the building of a railway bridge across the Thames, and, finally, the building of Charing Cross Station and its hotel. But between August 1859 and February 1864 the whole scheme was completed. Such was the effect of competitive enterprise in the railway battle for London.

Not content with this triumph—and, indeed, before it had been achieved—the South Eastern made a branch from its new line at Southwark and built another Thames bridge and a terminus right in the heart of the City, at Cannon Street (Fig. 25). Here again the station shed was fronted by a hotel.

In such hectic adventures as these one would not expect "high art" to find much of a place. Nor did it. Hawkshaw's iron girder bridges and the great hangars with their "sickle" roof trusses which formed the station sheds were ferociously utilitarian and without any of the grace of earlier engineering. In the hotels, however, where a tradition of luxurious appointment had been set, notably by Paddington and the Grosvenor at Victoria, art was needed. Both at Charing Cross and at Cannon Street, Edward Middleton Barry, the younger of Sir Charles's two architect sons, was called in to supply it. His Cannon Street hotel is gone, but the Charing Cross hotel survives and is still worth a visit for its handsome dining room and spacious Doric corridors. The front to the Strand has French roofs and was said to be François 1er, which is arguable. A somewhat eccentric gesture of liberality was made here by the railway company when they instructed Barry to build a quasi-fourteenth-century "Eleanor Cross" in the station yard to replace the Charing Cross destroyed in 1646.

The South Eastern's successes had not discouraged the London, Chatham and Dover, which by 1864 had built its own Thames bridge and a station at Ludgate Hill, after which it penetrated even further, building an iron bridge slap across the face of St. Paul's Cathedral and eventually landing up with a terminus and hotel at Holborn Viaduct in 1874.

The northern railway companies were in no such flurry of anxiety, and when in 1862 the highly successful Midland Railway decided to bring its lines to London and build a terminus between Euston and King's Cross the thing was done with a stateliness and amplitude more in the tradition of old Euston and Paddington. St. Pancras Station and hotel (now offices) are, I suppose, among the most famous railway monuments in the world. W. H. Barlow's iron shed, with its lattice ribs covering, in the shape of a four-centered arch, the then unheard-of span of 240 feet, commands immediate respect (Fig. 26). The hotel (Fig. 27), for which a limited competition was held, is the work of the leading Gothic revivalist, George Gilbert Scott. It has gathered respect in recent years almost in proportion to the loathing which was felt for it forty years ago. The contrast with the station shed is, of course, ludicrous and exacerbated by the exploitation of cathedral Gothic as, in the words of a contemporary, "an 'advertising medium' for bagmen's bedrooms and the costly

Fig. 25. The South Eastern railway terminus at Cannon
Street, City, 1865–66. The engineer for the bridge and
the station was John Hawkshaw.

INTERIOR OF THE NEW ST. PANCRAS STATION, MIDLAND RAILWAY.

Fig. 26. The Midland Railway terminus at St. Pancras, designed by W. H. Barlow, 1862.

Fig. 27. The Midland Railway hotel, St. Pancras, designed by George Gilbert Scott in 1868 in a mixture of English, French, Flemish, and Venetian Gothic.

Fig. 28. Detail of Holborn Viaduct, built by the City of London over the Fleet valley and completed in 1869.

discomforts of a railway hotel." But a certain brilliance in the whole performance cannot be denied.

St. Pancras Station and hotel stand at the peak of the railway construction era, which is also the period of maximum movement in London as a whole. Railways, roads, embankments, markets, and suburban developments all reacted on each other. The railways accelerated the flight from the City of its residential population and helped its reconstruction as an area for daily business only. The City had its own urgent problems in coming to terms with the new age. It rebuilt its markets: first the Metropolitan Cattle Market, for live beasts, in 1855; then the Smithfield Meat Market, for dead beasts, in 1867–68. In 1866 it faced the long-standing problem of bridging the Fleet valley by the construction of a viaduct connecting Holborn to Newgate Street and making straight and safe one of the main approaches to the City (Fig. 28). The viaduct was finished in 1869, in time for Queen Victoria to pass under it when she rode to open a new Thames road bridge promoted by the City to replace the classical bridge at Blackfriars with a massive combination of British iron, and stones, via Ruskin, of Venice.

The rebuilding of the City was one of the major phenomena of the sixties. We have seen how it started, with the banks and insurance companies jostling for place in the central area around the Royal Exchange. After 1857 the rebuilding greatly accelerated and the architecture became more adventurous. The norm of Barry's sober Italian did not always satisfy the craving for self-advertisement. Each insurance company wished to establish its own character, and the builders of office blocks wished at least to pretend that each new block had a prestige-bearing character of its own. The banks, naturally, preferred a more conservative image. The finest bank building in the City is the National Provincial, in Bishopsgate (Fig. 29). Designed by John Gibson, a pupil of Barry's, it takes Soane's Bank of England theme and deploys it richly and majestically. Scheduled for demolition a few years ago, this building has been saved by an ingenious compromise, involving a high-rise block on part of the site.

Ruskin's influence penetrated into City architecture from 1858 when Deane and Woodward, architects of the Oxford Museum, built the Crown Life office in New Bridge Street—Romanesque with naturalistic ornament (Fig. 30). The National Provident followed with a richly latitudinarian facade (Fig. 31) in 1863, and in 1868 came George Somers Clarke's extremely striking General Credit building in Lothbury (Fig. 32). Clarke, another pupil of Barry's, here put aside his master's tradition and brought the stones of medieval Venice to the very precincts of the Bank of England.

There were wilder outbreaks than this, such as the warehouse for a firm of vinegar manufacturers in Eastcheap by R. L. Roumieu, 1867. On the other hand there were some serious considerations of rational design, like George Aitchison's office block in Mark Lane of 1869, where an all-iron structure of rather advanced design was given a logical and subtly designed masonry front. By 1870 City architecture had become an intensely experimental field, and when the new artery called Queen Victoria Street, constructed (as we saw earlier) by the MBW, was opened in 1869 some very disturbing solutions of the office block problem made their appearance. A developer named Major Wieland, operating in this street, employed Frederick J. Ward to design Albert Buildings, an audacious attempt to make French Gothic forms fit the facts of multistory office-building (Fig. 33). On the other side of the street, in another Wieland enterprise, Ward played the same game with quattrocento Renaissance.

But the real surprise in the design of office buildings came in 1873 when a developing company brought in a rising architect named Richard Norman Shaw to design an office block called New Zealand Chambers in Leadenhall Street (Fig. 34). Shaw had nothing previously to do with the City. His patrons had been rich country landowners who wanted rambling, picturesque houses where to entertain, to shoot, to hunt, and to relax. Shaw's experience in this area of design, if it did not qualify him in any obvious sense to build office blocks, had given him a unique independence of stylistic prejudices. He had come to see that if neither the Italian school nor the Gothic revival had the flexibility required to solve Victorian problems, the despised vernacular of the seventeenth and early eighteenth century had. It had, besides, possibilities for new artistic effects. At New Zealand Chambers he took the old merchant style of Stuart London, with its ample, luminous bays and quaint ornament, and made a modern building out of it. Older architects were deeply shocked. Younger men hardly knew what to think. But from the moment of building New Zealand Chambers, Shaw took the lead in English architecture—the lead so long and so firmly held by Sir Charles Barry. Another thing about New Zealand Chambers was that the office suites it contained let quickly and at high rents.

Shaw's New Zealand House was an isolated phenomenon in the City; but, taken in another context, it was only one of many signs of the profound change in style and taste in English architecture which occurred around 1870. It is important to appreciate this change because it affected the whole color and architectural texture of London for the remainder of the century. It cannot be explained in terms of the architecture of the sixties which we have been looking at, in the City or elsewhere. Nearly all this was the product either of urgent public necessity or of competitive enterprise. Most of it was pretty crude. There are areas of building activity, however, of which I have as yet made no mention. These include church-building, mostly with pious intention, backed by wealth, in the poorer parts of London; and the building of a few major public buildings at the national expense, the architects for these being mostly selected in competition.

I place church-building first because, as I mentioned earlier, it was the area chiefly identified with the Gothic revival and therefore the one to which most architects of talent were drawn in the forties and fifties. This fact had curious repercussions in the public area later on. The London churches of the sixties do not make anything like the show made by the estate churches of the forties and fifties. The best of them are deliberately sited in stricken areas, where, it was believed, with more faith than realism, the combined ministration of charity, religious education, and the sacraments would be a means of relieving the miseries of the poor. Nevertheless, they are works of imagination and often great costliness. In their slum environments they were thought of as "lilies among weeds." Three outstanding works belong to the early sixties. Butterfield's St. Alban, Holborn (Fig. 35; destroyed, except for the west end, in World War II); Pearson's St. Peter, Vauxhall; and Street's St. James the Less, Thorn-

55

Fig. 29. The National Provincial Bank, Bishopsgate,
designed by John Gibson, a pupil of Barry's, in 1865.

Fig. 30. The Crown Life Insurance office, New Bridge Street, designed by Deane and Woodward in 1858 and demolished seven years later.

Fig. 31. The National Provident building, Gracechurch
Street, in the "latitudinarian" style of Robert Kerr,
1863 (demolished).

Fig. 32. The General Credit building, Lothbury, designed by George Somers Clarke, a pupil of Barry's, in 1868.

Fig. 33. Albert Buildings, Queen Victoria Street, 1869,
one of Major Wieland's office block speculations. His
architect was Frederick J. Ward.

dike Street (Fig. 36). All three are mostly of brick, the traditional London material (the showy churches of the fifties were
usually of stone); all three are sophisticated and original in
their handling of Gothic; all three have rich interior decorations.
They were followed by other fine churches by the same architects and by churches of similar quality by lesser men, such as
James Brooks, as well as by a miscellaneous host of far less honorable buildings.

The more dedicated Gothic revivalists, though necessarily
concerned mostly with churches, parsonages, and schools, sin-
cerely believed in the universal applicability of their style and
promoted its interest whenever they could. When in 1857 a
competition was held for the design of new government offices
in Whitehall, Scott, Street, and a few other Gothic men sent in
designs. The first places went to Italian or "modern French"
projects, but by an astonishing series of manipulations by the
Gothic lobby the awards were upset and Scott installed as architect. This was the famous "battle of the styles," which ended
only when Lord Palmerston, while accepting Scott as architect,
forced him into making an Italian design. Which, rather shame-
facedly, Scott did—and did very competently (Fig. 37).

Nine years later, in 1866, when the government had decided
to remove the law courts from Westminster and rebuild them
in the legal area of the Strand, came the competition for an even
more imposing building, the Royal Courts of Justice. This was a
limited competition among twelve leading architects. Inevitably,
at that moment all twelve men had Gothic running in their heads
and all the designs were Gothic. The least Gothic-minded, E. M.
Barry, whom we met as an architect of railway hotels, won the
competition on points, with Scott as runner-up. But once again
there was a rather scandalous reversal of judgment and the work
was given to Street. Street's building (Fig. 38) was begun in
1873; the great hall, a supremely noble vaulted nave, was finished
in 1876. But the law courts are, on the whole, a heroic failure.
The Gothic revival, with its strong ecclesiastical roots, could not
identify itself, either psychologically or technologically, with the
crude secular programs of high Victorianism. Scott had tried, as
we have seen, to achieve such an identification at St. Pancras
hotel with a result which, set against the station shed, was seen

Fig. 34. New Zealand Chambers, Leadenhall Street, 1873 (demolished), where Richard Norman Shaw revived the City vernacular of the seventeenth century.

Fig. 35. St. Alban, Holborn, William Butterfield's
church of 1862–63. Only the west end (above) survived
rebuilding after World War II.

63

Fig. 36. St. James the Less, Thorndike Street, designed by George Edmund Street, 1860–61. Model is preserved in the church.

Fig. 37. Government offices, Whitehall, seen from St. James's Park; designed by George Gilbert Scott and Matthew Digby Wyatt, 1868–73.

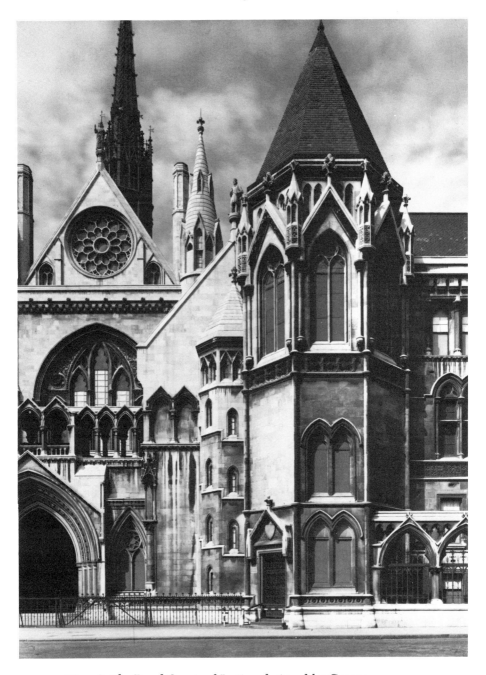

Fig. 38. The Royal Courts of Justice, designed by George
Edmund Street and begun in 1873; detail of the entrance
in the Strand.

to be ludicrous and vulgar. Street's law courts are neither ludicrous nor vulgar. Against their inconsistencies and anachronisms can be set many beauties. But they are at war with their function, socially and structurally, as a younger generation of architects saw very clearly. Richard Norman Shaw, a pupil of Street's, was one of that generation.

Public works, in the sense of great official buildings, are not a dominating feature of Victorian London, and it is natural that they should not be. In an economy running with such miraculous success on the laissez-faire principle, action by the government and expenditure by the government were always suspect, always opposed. The government, it was believed, should do as little as possible and spend as little as possible. Nevertheless, there was one area where public works were initiated and carried on, largely at the public expense and for no more practical reason than the encouragement of public interest in the arts and sciences. That area was South Kensington.

The South Kensington story is curiously insulated from other spheres of development in the period. The incentives, the aims and objects, the procedures, and even the architectural styles involved have a character entirely their own. It all started with the Great Exhibition of 1851, and, perhaps one should add, with the patronage of Prince Albert and all that that implies in the way of German attitudes and influences. When the Exhibition closed there was a very substantial surplus in the hands of the commissioners. This surplus they proceeded to spend on a piece of South Kensington property amounting to about eighty-six acres, to be dedicated principally to cultural purposes. What these purposes were was at first doubtful, but in 1856 the government bought twelve acres in one corner of the site on which to build some temporary iron buildings to house the collection of works of art already assembled for educational purposes by the Department of Science and Art. These iron buildings, which got nicknamed the "Brompton boilers," were the beginnings of the Victoria and Albert Museum. In 1858 a new gallery was added to the "boilers," and the designer of this was not an architect but a young officer in the Royal Engineers, Capt. Francis Fowke, who was to figure as the architectural genius of South Kensington until his early death in 1865. In 1860 Fowke made outline plans for a completely new art museum, but these were not developed till after his death.

Meanwhile, in 1859 a main portion of the South Kensington site was leased to the Royal Horticultural Society, who, with government subsidies, formed a very elaborate garden and surrounded it with architectural arcades and pavilions on three sides and a big iron conservatory on the fourth. Fowke had a share of the design, and it is here that we see the beginnings of the South Kensington style. The style is a curious mixture of historicism and modernism. The historicism involves a keen interest in North Italian terra-cotta and faience. The modernism is involved with iron, treated structurally and decoratively as in the Crystal Palace.

The next things to come on the South Kensington site were the buildings for the International Exhibition of 1862. These, again, were by Fowke and included a great iron and timber nave with iron-domed spaces at each end. When the exhibition was over, the site of these buildings was designated for another museum, the British Museum of Natural History, which was to house and supplement the natural history exhibits then grossly overcrowded in the old British Museum in Bloomsbury. It was thought improper to hand this great new commission directly to Fowke. An open competition was therefore held. A panel of impartial judges awarded the prize—to Fowke! If he had not died two years later, the Natural History Museum would have been built to his designs. To the building actually built we shall come later.

By this time, other projects were developing. The Prince Consort, who had taken so great a share in all the South Kensington proceedings, had died in 1861. Naturally the question of memorials arose, and South Kensington seemed the appropriate place for some of them. Two memorials emerged. The first, what is called the Albert Memorial (Fig. 39), consists of a vast Gothic canopy rising over a seated effigy of the Prince and is sited in Hyde Park on the axis of the Horticultural Gardens. The second, the Albert Hall, is situated opposite the memorial and nearly on the same axis.

The design for the Albert Memorial issued from an informal competition among seven architects. There was only one assessor

Fig. 39. The Albert Memorial, designed by George Gilbert
Scott on the model of a medieval shrine or reliquary
and completed in 1869.

Fig. 40. The Albert Hall, designed by Captain Fowke of the Royal Engineers and completed after Fowke's death by General Scott. Queen Victoria opened it in 1871.

—the Queen—and she chose Sir Gilbert Scott's design. The memorial, which has been mercilessly treated by critics, has magnificent scale and sweep. Scott himself explained it as a medieval shrine or reliquary magnified to the "natural" scale of which such objects seem to be miniatures. The memorial, paid for by public subscription supplemented by a parliamentary grant, was finished in 1869. By this time the Albert Hall, opposite, was well advanced.

The curious thing about the Albert Hall (Fig. 40) is that nobody at the time knew exactly what it was to be for. The chief motivator of the scheme was Sir Henry Cole—the busy promoter of so many things in the art and art education of his day. He believed, without much evidence, that the idea of a great hall dedicated to the arts and sciences had been a favorite of Prince Albert's. That was the starting point. From there, a private company took over to handle the thing on a business footing without expecting much in the way of dividends. Designs by various architects were submitted; Cole, however, distrusted architects and preferred military engineers. Some sketches were made by Captain Fowke before his death; after that his design was developed by Colonel (later General) Scott, with an architect only for the decorative details, which were, of course, in brick, terracotta, and faience, with a North Italian flavor. The idea was that of a Roman amphitheater, but one covered by an iron-structured dome; and the dome construction by R. M. Ordish is perhaps the most thrilling part of the building. The Albert Hall was opened by the Queen in 1871.

By this date the South Kensington precinct was really beginning to take shape. There was the Albert Memorial on the north, then the Albert Hall, then a platform and steps leading down to the Horticultural Society's garden, then the 1862 Exhibition buildings, still standing but about to be demolished. On a site to the east, the buildings of the South Kensington Museum were beginning to rise. That great enterprise was not to be completed for another forty years, and it is only the beginnings which concern us here. They include the main courtyard, a perfect example of the Fowke style, in brick and terra-cotta, and the remarkable South Court, a sort of miniature Paddington Station dedicated to art and the quintessence of all we mean when we say South Kensington.

There we must leave South Kensington for the present. Far more was to be built—far too much more—on that famous site, and to some of the additions I shall need to return. But in closing my account of London in the two critical decades between 1857 and 1877 I want to return momentarily to the subject of architectural taste, so vital a factor in the visual image of any great city. You will recall that in speaking of Norman Shaw's New Zealand Chambers, I observed that the building represented a profound change of attitude to architectural design which was not noticeable in the other buildings with which I had been dealing. Nor was it noticeable at South Kensington. Whence came this change and what was its nature? It showed first in the private houses of men, not necessarily of great wealth, who were either artists or patrons of the arts. It became effective among young architects who were neither caught up in the whirl of commercial and industrial building nor necessarily dedicated to the building of Gothic churches. It became a movement developing out of the Gothic revival, much modified by Ruskin's writings but turning away from the revival toward a freer philosophy of design. Out of it emerged the fairly distinct style of ornamental brick-building which, absurdly, was nicknamed "Queen Anne"—though another, more vivid and less elegant name was "re-renaissance." It was in the "Queen Anne" style that many of the hundreds of schools resulting from the great Education Act of 1870 were built. This was no accident. New freedoms and simplicity in design went along with a new concern for social questions and less impregnable assumptions about the hierarchies of class. It is to the emergence of this style and its exposition in some of the buildings of London through the eighties and nineties that I shall direct your attention next.

3

The change of taste which manifested itself in London architecture from about the year 1870 and which gradually changed the color and textural character of London through the next three decades did not lead to any particular style—except, indeed, the "Queen Anne." "Queen Anne" in this context, may mean almost anything from late medieval Flemish to François 1ᵉʳ, but more especially an eclectic mixture of vernacular English seventeenth-century red brick and tall eighteenth-century sash windows, with a Pre-Raphaelite sunflower or two, cut in brick, as the chief decoration. This new taste has its beginnings in some of the inner suburbs of London in a series of houses built in the sixties and seventies. I think we may call them "artistic" houses. They were built either for artists or for people with strong interest in the arts and happy to break away from the overwhelming conventionality of the London house of the previous era. Already by 1880 these "artistic" houses were thought of as an interesting and important series.

For the first of these houses we have to go to Holland Park, then still a domain of parkland on the western fringe of Kensington. Here, Philip Webb, in 1864, built a very small house with very big studio windows for the young painter Val Prinsep. Webb had, five years earlier, built the Red House at Bexley for his friend William Morris. Prinsep's house, like Morris's, was free of definable stylistic affiliations, simple and modest. Four years later than the Prinsep house, Webb built a little house at Chelsea for Rossetti's friend G. P. Boyce, which is an almost complete reversion to Georgian. About the same time, he built a much bigger house in Palace Green, Kensington, for the wealthy amateur George Howard, later Earl of Carlisle (Fig. 41). In this house of 1868, Webb showed much more strongly his inventive and original mind, bringing together motifs and moldings of different kinds whose sources one looks for in vain because they have been transmuted by Webb's curiously private and abstruse sensitivity. This house was never much publicized (Webb loathed publicity) and was perhaps too subtle for the general, but in 1870 a Scottish architect, J. J. Stevenson, built himself a house in Bayswater Road (only a short walk from Palace Green; Fig.

42), which, I think, may fairly be seen as a vulgarization of Webb. This house received a great deal of publicity (Stevenson loved publicity) and was always regarded as the first real manifestation of "Queen Anne." Its mixture of simple brick ornaments and sash windows was soon being imitated all over London. It was, of course, mostly red brick, and the house was, like Morris's at Bexley, called the Red House. It was blasted in World War II and later demolished.

There followed in 1873, on the other side of the park, a much larger house which obviously owes much to Stevenson's. This is Lowther Lodge, Kensington, built for the Earl of Lonsdale by Richard Norman Shaw (Fig. 43). Shaw was then forty-four. He had made his reputation with huge, dramatically picturesque, country houses and had only one previous work in London—the shockingly picturesque and countrified New Zealand Chambers in the City (see p. 53). Lowther Lodge is really a country house—as near into London as a new country house could get and right on the fringe of the great South Kensington operations I described earlier. It revolted against the stiff palisades of stucco frontage of which most of South Kensington consisted—and the revolt was welcome.

After Lowther Lodge, Shaw built one or more London houses, either in Kensington, Chelsea, or Hampstead, every year up to 1890, and a remarkable series they are. They were all for rich men, some of them artists. At a lower income level, smaller artists were able to build themselves houses in the better suburbs; and a series built in Hampstead in the seventies by the architects Batterbury and Huxley illustrates well the changing taste of a sophisticated but not rich section of society. The series starts in Steele's Road with houses still gabled, with decorative bargeboards, but also with sash windows. Then the gable is replaced by a hipped roof and there is a nice classical doorframe done in Georgian-type brick. In Hampstead Hill Gardens the series continues with quite elegant early Georgian types showing the extent to which, in some circles, the Gothic revival had become completely outdated. A classical revival was on the way—always, however, with a strong vernacular tinge.

Such houses are, of course, exceptional in the suburbia of the seventies and eighties; Hampstead was always rather special. Of suburbia in general after 1870 I do not propose to say much. There was a total change in the character of expanding London with the coming of suburban railways. No longer were suburbs fringe areas, fanning out from the central mass of London into the country within the range that horsedrawn traffic could conveniently serve them. They were blotches of building enterprise, fed by the stations, each blotch expanding to meet the next blotch along the line. These are the "dormitory suburbs" of late Victorian London. They were created because high rents in the center, in combination with cheap rail fares and the understandable desire to escape for at least half one's living hours from smoke and fog, made them desirable to a large section of lower-middle-class people. The shape of these suburbs was determined by the complex and uncoordinated operation of thousands of small builders. The leasehold system prevailed, but not on the dignified and orderly lines on which we saw it at work in Bayswater and Kensington. Landowners saw no future in sophisticated planning of their estates. No affluent house-hunters were to be attracted, and the profits to be had were meager. There was no effective control of building in these areas, and land was laid out and sewered according to the short-term prospects of very small operators. As to the architectural results, a characteristic vernacular evolved, still basically Georgian but faintly and sometimes grotesquely tinged by fashionable ideas filtering down from the architectural world of the West End. The whole object of the builders of these houses was to sell or rent quick and avoid bankruptcy. The bay window with twisted pillars and the carved head over the door were devices of salesmanship, symbols of "class," to give confidence to the house-hunting clerk or shop assistant. The subject of the Victorian suburban vernacular, seen from this angle, is not without interest and is wide open to anybody with the necessary stamina to investigate it.

Against this background, the idea of actually *creating* a suburb instead of letting it come about through a multiplicity of uncoordinated agencies never ceased entirely to be cherished. A few enlightened landowners of the forties did lay out suburban properties with a distinct idea of creating a community or, at least, a neighborhood; but such ideas tended to crumble at the first economic setback. The idea of working-class commuters' villages

75

Fig. 41. Detail of the house in Palace Green, Kensington,
built by Philip Webb for the Honorable George Howard
in 1868.

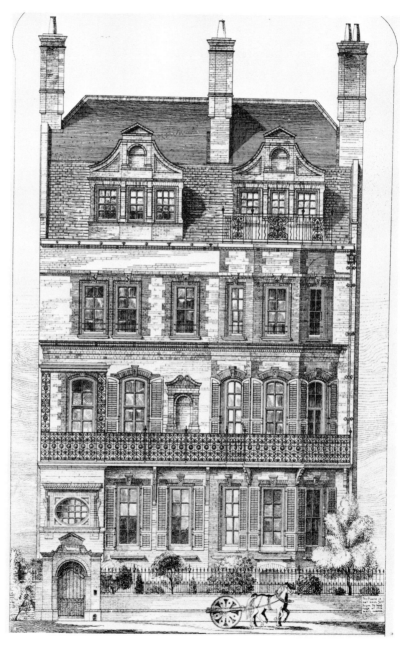

Fig. 42. The Red House, Bayswater Road, Paddington,
built for himself by J. J. Stevenson in 1870 (demolished).

Fig. 43. Lowther Lodge, Kensington, built by Richard
Norman Shaw for the Earl of Lonsdale in 1873.

Fig. 44. House on the Lavender Hill estate of the
Artisans, Labourers and General Dwellings Company,
formed in 1867.

was also proposed from time to time and made some real progress in the hands of a quasi-philanthropic body called the Artisans, Labourers and General Dwellings Company (Fig. 44). The company was founded under the aegis of Lord Shaftesbury in 1867 with the idea of enabling working men to erect dwellings and become the owners of them. Three estates were developed in the course of the seventies, with regular streets of substantial houses, neat and solid enough but singularly lacking in any sense of suburban amenity. Then, in the mid-seventies came Bedford Park.

Bedford Park was a country estate lying about five miles west of Hyde Park Corner. Early in the seventies it was acquired by Jonathan Carr, a man involved with various building projects and exceptional in his interest in social and artistic matters. Perhaps through his brother, an art critic, he knew something of William Morris and the Pre-Raphaelite circle. At Bedford Park, Carr proposed to create a middle-class suburb of a kind which that circle could approve—simple, modest, but "artistic," relying much on well-chosen materials and the preservation of trees. He took Norman Shaw as his architect, though the first houses were built (rather badly) from a design by E. W. Godwin, and other architects were also involved. Norman Shaw designed the church in a wonderfully felicitous mixture of late Gothic and seventeenth-century vernacular; also the Tabard Inn (the sign is evocative of Chaucer) and some of the houses. Bedford Park, begun in 1875, developed through the late seventies and eighties without in any way betraying its founder's ideals. At first regarded as quaint and "arty" because of the cozy style of its red-brick and red-tiled houses, Bedford Park gave the model for many of the suburban types which prevailed well into the twentieth century. But the point of Bedford Park was the coherence of its conception as a neighborhood. It was the first Garden City.

The change of taste which is so noticeable here and in some other products of London building comes just at the time when attitudes to social questions, especially in the great cities and most especially in London, are beginning to change. Changes in taste and changes in attitudes to social questions are not, by any means, necessarily connected; and they were not connected in the minds of most Londoners of the seventies. Yet there is one remarkable instance where a connection can be demonstrated and that is in the school buildings of the London School Board.

The great Elementary Education Act, passed in 1870, laid down lines upon which education should be provided wherever it was inadequately served; but in the case of London, the act directed the setting up of a London School Board which should proceed at once with the building of whatever number of schools were necessary for the reception of all children not already attending school. Schools did, of course, exist in London, in large numbers. All of them had religious affiliations. Most of them were church schools, built by voluntary subscriptions, with tiny grants-in-aid from public funds. With the coming of the act this was changed. A huge building campaign, to be paid for out of rates, was organized to supply as soon as possible buildings for 112,000 children.

The board set itself up in a grand headquarters on the new Victoria Embankment. It proceeded to appoint a school architect, and the man chosen was E. R. Robson. Robson was not only an architect of ability but one of sufficient imagination to see the greatness of his task. While the average educated Londoner of the time thought of board schools as squalid necessities on which as little of their money as possible should be spent, Robson saw two things very clearly: first, the complexity of the functional problems to be solved and, second, the need for a mode of expression which should be uniquely appropriate to these new buildings. Now Robson, in his private sphere, was in partnership with J. J. Stevenson, whose Red House, in Bayswater Road, we saw to have been the first exposition of what was called the "Queen Anne" style. In the new schools, where heating, lighting, hygiene, and ventilation were treated with great seriousness, the "Queen Anne," with its flexibility of disposition and its happy use of common materials, found its truest destination.

Not all the schools were "Queen Anne"—some were by architects still rather faintheartedly guarding the Gothic principle. But the influence of Robson and of Stevenson prevailed, and the best of their schools are among the most enlightened buildings of their time. The Robson type of school (Fig. 45) became, through the seventies and eighties, one of the characteristic features of the London scene, its tall curving long-windowed gables

Fig. 45. School in Wornington Road, Kensington,
designed by the architect to the London School Board,
E. R. Robson, 1872 (demolished).

rising above the London rooftops in rivalry with the gin palaces and the churches. Robson's schools are now out of date and disappearing fast or being converted to other uses. As a component of late Victorian London they are not to be forgotten.

It is strange, on the face of it, that no other type of building emerges from the seventies with the same consistency as the board schools. The reason is that neither in the sphere of public health nor in that of housing was there any legislation which imposed on anybody the duty of building anything, though we should perhaps except the Metropolitan Poor Act of 1867, with its progeny of bleak, grey infirmaries in a minimal Gothic. Both in health and housing the voluntary principle was maintained till the end of the century.

Nevertheless, in studying late Victorian London architecture it is inevitable that we think in terms of building *types*. From the seventies onward we are no longer in a period of urban extension (the far-flung dormitory suburbs are another thing), nor yet of structural alteration in the sense of highway and railroad building—that was all over by 1880—but in a period of redevelopment by filling in or by replacement on the existing map. This means that even buildings of social or representative consequence had to find sites where they could, and by pulling down something else. To give two examples: both the Roman Catholic Cathedral at Westminster and the Tate Gallery were built on the sites of obsolete prisons. This process had gone far, by the end of the century, to efface the Georgian character of the capital and to give it the bewilderingly miscellaneous image which it still wears. This image is the composite of very many diverse types. These were rarely absolutely new types but developments and elaborations and subdivisions of types more simply stated years before. Elaboration from the simple to the complex in plan, in construction and technical equipment, and, indeed, in architectural handling is characteristic of the eighties and nineties. The architect found himself assailed by a host of technological novelties and improvements—in heating, ventilation, sanitation, and fire protection. More than that, he found that in a general practice he would be called on to handle many different types, each with its own very special considerations. Alfred Waterhouse made this point in 1883 in a speech arguing that "style" had become more important than "the styles" in an age when the architect was employed not merely on town and country houses, city buildings, churches, and the occasional public building, but on "concert rooms, theatres, town-halls, courts of justice, government offices, museums, picture-galleries, hospitals, palaces, clubhouses, hotels, colleges, public schools and other educational buildings"; to which he might have added stores, branch banks, public baths, public libraries, restaurants, taverns, and blocks of flats—and, indeed, a great deal else.

This proliferation of types makes the description of late Victorian London a difficult business; nor is it made any easier by the proliferation of architectural styles. The "Queen Anne" movement of the seventies was only a first step toward a renewed interest in all the early Renaissance styles of the sixteenth and early seventeenth centuries—French, Flemish, Dutch, and Spanish; side by side of which ran the classical tradition, which, however, had come to be interpreted and vulgarized rather as modern French. The Gothic styles still held a little ground, in church-building fairly consistently, but also, in various late and linear forms, in street architecture. Much of the architecture is, of course, at a desperately low level. The profession was undereducated and wide open to people who were not architects at all but builders, developers, or surveyors whose designs were made for them by a pathetic race of "ghosts." The effective architects—those who by their works and influence really changed the character and color of London—were relatively few. The leader certainly was Richard Norman Shaw, whose personality bestrides late Victorian London just as Sir Charles Barry's bestrode the early Victorian scene. Almost exact contemporaries of Shaw were Philip Webb, that remote and saintly innovator; J. J. Stevenson, of "Queen Anne" fame; and Waterhouse, with his harsh originalities. Ten years younger was another "constellation" of architects —Ernest George, R. W. Edis, and T. E. Collcutt, all cultivating Renaissance manners and all more or less influenced by Shaw. These architects powerfully changed the visual image of London. They changed its style through their new attitudes to the past. They changed its color by changing its materials from brown brick to brown and red, then to red; from Portland stone to granite or reddish Mansfield or to red or buff terra-cotta. An analysis of the whole architectural content of London in 1901 would show an enormous indebtedness to these names.

Such an analysis would be a monumental undertaking, not even to be adumbrated within the present framework. All I can do by way of conclusion is to attempt to demonstrate something of the sheer complexity and richness of London in the last two Victorian decades by passing under swift review the principal sectors of building activity, flashing an occasional light on buildings of special quality or consequence.

Take first the London house. By 1877 estate development in the central areas had come almost to an end. The ground was covered and only a few freakish vacancies remained. Two of these were on the Cadogan estate, where Cadogan Square was built in the course of the eighties, and on the Harrington estate, where Harrington Gardens and Collingham Gardens were built during the same period. The great stucco regiments of Bayswater and South Kensington were now despised, and in these later enterprises "Queen Anne" and the renaissances took over, Norman Shaw and J. J. Stevenson playing conspicuous parts in Cadogan Square and Ernest George creating in Collingham Gardens (Fig. 46) a plausible reflection of the Amsterdam of Pieter de Hoogh. Another enclave of "Queen Anne" development is that created by J. J. Stevenson at Kensington Court, on the site of a demolished mansion. All these represent the last collective flowering of the London house. By the time they were finished there were no more vacant sites in areas fashionable enough for such initiatives. Town houses of the future would be rebuildings on Georgian sites, and there would not be many; by 1890 London was beginning to be rebuilt not in houses but in blocks of flats.

The earliest middle-class flats were, as we have seen, those of 1852 in Victoria Street. They were followed by the socially and economically more successful Belgrave Mansions, only a hundred yards away but on the aristocratic Grosvenor estate, in 1867. After that, the Victoria Street area became peculiarly susceptible to flat-building, and in 1874–77 a ruthless developer named Hankey took advantage of the then perfected hydraulic lift, and the absence of statutory restrictions as to height, to raise a block fourteen stories high, called Queen Anne's Mansions, a little northward of the street. It was a wholly utilitarian structure, causing much distress to Queen Victoria and causing no distress to anybody when it was demolished in 1971.

Five years after this, a syndicate took a large vacant site just east of the Albert Hall, on ground belonging to the Commissioners for the 1851 Exhibition, and employed Norman Shaw to build a monster block of flats of a new kind, to be called Albert Hall Mansions (Fig. 47). With wonderful courage and invention Shaw planned a building with split levels to give lofty drawing rooms toward the park and lower rooms at the back and marshaled the resources of "Queen Anne" to make a highly picturesque ensemble. This was the first and also the last time in the Victorian period that the new problem of flat-building came into the hands of a major architect. We may concede that in the next monster block, Whitehall Court on the Victoria Embankment (Fig. 21), the firm of Archer and Green handled the problem without disgrace and with some skill in the marriage of "Queen Anne" to François 1ᵉʳ, whose Château de Madrid, as recorded by du Cerçeau, seems to be the inspiration. The later monster blocks are not merely without distinction but hasty and vulgar concoctions by architects of a very low type working with builders who were often themselves the developers. Carlyle Mansions, Chelsea, is just mildly grim. St. James's Court of 1899 is an example of maximum exploitation of very expensive building land producing destructive and horrible results (Fig. 48). The trouble about flats at this period was that they depended for success on a good address. The snob name "St. James's Court" for a building nowhere near St. James's is typical. Suburban flats were almost unknown, except in Battersea, till after 1900. Outside London there were none. So investment in flat-building meant grabbing central sites and piling onto them as much as the building acts and the ground landlords would allow. In 1881 the Georgian integrity of Portland Place was first invaded. In 1882 flats came to Berkeley Square. In the nineties, Cavendish, Hanover, and Kensington squares were broken into. The destruction of Georgian London had begun in earnest.

More sweeping changes in the visual aspect of London came with development in the general category of "business premises" and the creation of the great shopping areas of the West End. In the City itself, after the headlong rebuilding of 1855–75, there

Fig. 46. Collingham Gardens, Kensington; houses
designed ca. 1881 by Ernest George and Peto.

Fig. 47. Albert Hall Mansions, Kensington, 1879, the first block of London flats to be built to designs by a major architect, Richard Norman Shaw.

was a pause. Nearly all the prestige streets were filled up with Italian or sometimes Gothic facades, and the construction of Queen Victoria Street and Holborn Viaduct temporarily over-supplied the City with vacant sites. The typical City building of the last quarter of the century is the block of lettable office or warehouse space. This was not a new type in principle, but in the new streets and some of the old it came into its own. Shaw's New Zealand Chambers of 1872, as we have seen, exploded the old stylistic conventions, and the various renaissances took the field. Ernest George, rebuilding part of Cheapside after a fire in 1882, introduced old Flemish, evocative of Bruges (Fig. 49). Collcutt brought his accomplished plateresque to Ludgate Hill in 1897. But the real City architects were practitioners of a lower order of talent, like Ford and Hesketh, Delissa Joseph, and T. E. Knightley, who framed remorselessly practical fenestrations within the thinnest possible slivers of Renaissance art, mostly of French derivation. In City office-building, as in West End flat-building, the period ends with an alarming explosion of sheer bulk. Winchester House, Old Broad Street, in a gruesome mod-ern French, dates from 1886, but the really stunning conclusion came with Salisbury House in Finsbury Circus. It contained 800 offices in eleven stories, with four staircases and seven lifts, and was completed in 1900.

It was in the seventies and eighties that rebuilding for business began to spread into the West. Successful shopkeepers who had expanded their premises by buying up adjoining houses, some-times to the extent of a whole block, found it expedient to re-build, partly for convenience and prestige, partly with an eye to subletting upper floors as offices. Marshall and Snelgrove, the drapers, rebuilt a whole block in Oxford Street as early as 1876, but rather drearily, in grey brick and stone, with conventional French roofs and ornaments. It was torn down in 1971. In the late seventies the new shapes and colors began to arrive. In Bond Street, the quaint windows of Norman Shaw's New Zealand Chambers found a ready imitator in 1877, and in the same year Robert Edis rebuilt a shop at the corner of New Bond Street and Brook Street (Fig. 50) with a red tile-hung gable, the first of its kind in London and shockingly unconventional. In Piccadilly, which had come to possess a soberly institutional character, Waterhouse's shop at the corner of Bond Street, gay with terra-cotta ornament, must have dazzled in 1880. Wigmore Street was transformed in terms of Flemish brick and terra-cotta, mostly by Ernest George and T. E. Collcutt. Changes on the Grosvenor estate were still more striking. Most of the Oxford Street frontages were rebuilt in the eighties as mixed business premises— shops below, offices above, all in some version of French Renaissance, with tourelles at the angles. On the southern boundary the run-down Mount Street area was entirely redeveloped between 1880 and 1890 in the liveliest brick and terra-cotta and in a happy variety of renaissances–François 1er by Ernest George, "Queen Anne" by Wimperis, Elizabethan by Verity, and, round the corner in Duke Street, Flemish by W. D. Caröe (Fig. 51). Nowhere can the quality architecture of the Victorian West End be better observed.

The residential and the business sectors very naturally take the biggest share of the building products of a society to which home life and making money were so very much the most important things. To probe the contents of other sectors would make this paper too long, but to establish what I mean by the complexity and elaboration of the period I must at least mention them. There are such important investment projects as theaters, hotels, and restaurants. The construction of Shaftesbury Avenue and Charing Cross Road (the last efforts of the MBW) attracted theatrical adventurers to the extent that at least one new theater was built every year through the eighties: a shoddy lot as architecture, except for Collcutt's involvement in the D'Oyly Carte's British Opera House (now the Palace Theatre; Fig. 52) and the swirling art nouveau auditorium of Daly's. It is extraordinary how little English theater design (or the English theater for that matter) developed between the Regency and 1900. Hotels, on the other hand, with no tradition behind them, developed in grand style after the railway series had set the pace. J. T. Knowles's Grosvenor and E. M. Barry's at Charing Cross and Cannon Street we have already noticed. As late as 1897 the Hotel Cecil and the Russell were thought out on similar but elaborated lines. But there were other approaches, and the hotel story is richly complex. So is the restaurant story, which starts with the rationalized chophouse, Pimm's, in the Poultry, 1870 (Fig. 53), for City peo-

Fig. 48. St. James's Court, Buckingham Gate, 1899, a monster block of flats with a good address. The architect was C. J. C. Pawley.

Fig. 49. Premises in Cheapside, City, designed by Ernest
George and Peto, 1882, to replace Georgian buildings
destroyed by fire (demolished).

Fig. 50. Shop in New Bond Street by Robert W. Edis, 1877 (demolished). The tile-hung gables were a striking innovation in the still almost wholly Georgian West End.

Fig. 51. Buildings in Duke Street, Mayfair, by W. D. Caröe, 1891, with (right) Alfred Waterhouse's King's Weigh-house Chapel of 1889–91.

ple, and proceeds with the highly complex enterprise of Spiers and Pond four years later at the Criterion (Fig. 54), where Thomas Verity enclosed behind his Renaissance facade a whole world of dining halls, grills, bars and buffets, dives and saloons, with a picture gallery at the top and a theater seating 1,500 (and still intact) in the basement. The great restaurants of the eighties and nineties—the Holborn, Romano's, Frascati's, and the Trocadero—never quite competed with this.

The institutional sector must not be overlooked since it includes the new type of men's club, like the St. Stephen's and National Liberal and the Constitutional, grown to the size of hotels and serving much the same purpose. It includes another almost new type—the professional institute headquarters: like Waterhouse's building for the Surveyors in Great George Street and that breathtaking innovation, the Institute of Chartered Accountants, 1894, where John Belcher, with Beresford Pite at his elbow, passed dramatically from re-renaissance to high baroque.

There are two sectors of activity which, though by no means unimportant, show after 1875 a reduction in initiative from the previous period. One is church-building. The other is building from religious-philanthropic motives generally. As to church-building, more churches were built in London in the seventies than in any other decade: an average of eleven new churches every year. But church-building owed its momentum to the enthusiasms of the fifties and sixties, and if the harvest of the seventies included the most mature works of Butterfield, Pearson, and Street, it was otherwise of indifferent quality. In the eighties the average dropped from eleven to eight, in the nineties from eight to four. It was not only that fewer churches were needed. People were worrying less about the restoration of faith and more about the conditions in which the faith was expected to flourish. The trouble with the poor, in short, was poverty rather than irreligion. Hence the decline in philanthropy of the Robert Brett and Baroness Burdett-Coutts kind—Christian missionaries bearing Gothic gifts. Earnestness in church design also dissolved into a search for atmospheric effect and artistic craftsmanship. The representative London church of the last years of the century is the rich and fashionable Holy Trinity, Sloane Street (consecrated 1890; Fig. 55), where the architect J. D. Sedding abandoned

Fig. 52. The Palace Theatre, Cambridge Circus, built for
D'Oyly Carte as the British Opera House, 1890. The
architect was T. E. Collcutt.

himself to the most sensuous devices of late Gothic and brought
in a varied team of artists to enrich the fabric in their own artistic
fashions. It is a church as revolutionary in its way as Butterfield's
All Saints, Margaret Street, but revolutionary in precisely the opposite direction—not from soft to hard but from hard to soft.

A more spectacular break with church-building of the past
was the commencement in 1894 of the Roman Catholic Cathedral
at Westminster (Fig. 56), built by a Gothic architect, John Francis Bentley, in a style which, although generally called Byzantine,
is really an extraordinary fusion of Gothic revival themes with
early Christian, Romanesque, and even Renaissance taste. It is
difficult to think of the building as Victorian.

While religious-philanthropic motives tended to become dim-
mer, the problems that created them were coming to be more
realistically examined. Housing the poor was the chief of these
problems. Gallant efforts had been made from the forties onward,
especially in the model housing projects of Henry Roberts. Then,
in 1862, came George Peabody's great donation, which resulted
over the years in the establishment of what was nothing less than
a quasi-public subsidized housing authority (Fig. 57). Sydney
Waterlow's Improved Industrial Dwellings Company of 1863 inaugurated what was called "5 per cent philanthropy," in other
words a type of development yielding modest returns with some
coloring of social benefaction. Other companies promoted this
kind of building, and specimens are widely dispersed throughout central London, often in the less potentially profitable
corners of fashionable areas. If the resulting buildings added
nothing to London's picturesque amenities (think of Charing
Cross Road!), they formed a bridge between the vague idealism
of the philanthropic pioneers and the assumption of responsibility
by public bodies—notably, in our case, by the London County
Council, whose first slum clearance and rehousing schemes belong
to 1896.

The building responsibilities of public bodies contributed to
late Victorian London some of its more significant—though not
necessarily more conspicuous—architectural contents. We have
already seen how the great Education Act of 1870 promoted a
new type of building, functionally and stylistically different from
earlier school buildings. Both output and quality were well main-

Fig. 53. Pimm's famous chop-house in the Poultry
(scheduled for demolition) includes the typical Georgian
front on the right and the 1870 extension designed by
R. H. Moore.

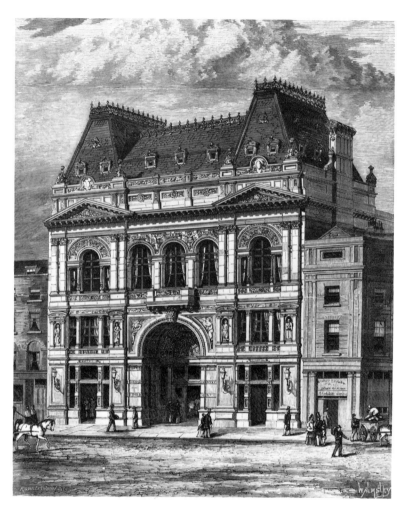

Fig. 54. The Criterion, Piccadilly Circus, 1874, designed
by Thomas Verity to comprise restaurants, bars, a picture
gallery, and, in the basement, a theater.

Fig. 55. Holy Trinity, Sloane Street, designed by J. D. Sedding, 1888–91, with the cooperation of the leading artist-craftsmen of the time.

Fig. 56. The Roman Catholic Cathedral, Westminster,
by John Francis Bentley, begun in 1894 and completed in
1903.

tained. In thirty-three years the London School Board built 500 schools at a cost of £14 million. Robson's "Queen Anne" style, somewhat coarsened in detail under his successor, persisted; but the board school, like so much else in late Victorian London, eventually exploded into sheer size—the Hugh Myddelton School in Clerkenwell (1892) for 2,000 children overloading its site nearly as oppressively as some offices and flats. Like any developer, the education authority had to get itself onto the map where it could and make the most of what it got.

In education, the nineties saw the opening of a new chapter. Twenty years of compulsory education created a demand for more education, and this was met by the polytechnic movement. Originating in philanthropic effort, the polytechnics were eventually paid for by the rolling up of antiquated charities by the charity commissioners *plus* a share of whiskey duty from the Exchequer through the London County Council. Each polytechnic institution managed its own affairs, and through the nineties each built for itself a building of a more or less collegiate kind, finding its architect through public competitions—occasions which the profession felt to be a challenge to find a new interpretation to match a new idea. Not all the results were brilliant, but some were. E. W. Mountford at the Battersea Polytechnic (1891) and again at the Northampton Institute in Islington (1893; Fig. 58) scored resounding successes with well-grouped compositions, basically "Queen Anne" but with something of the new feeling for Byzantine rhythm and silhouette which is an element in fin de siècle modernity. Modernity of a slightly different kind, probably influenced by America's H. H. Richardson, is expressed in Harrison Townsend's Bishopsgate Institute of 1894.

London's local authorities—the vestries of those parishes which became metropolitan boroughs in 1900, were not overloaded with building responsibility, but there were things for which they could borrow money to build if prodded into so doing by their electors. From 1846 they had, like the provincial municipalities, powers to build public baths and washhouses, and from 1850, free public libraries. These powers were scarcely used in London, however, until the eighties. The idea of public baths had been to raise the standard of hygiene among the grubbier sections of the population: some excellent installations were put up in the forties, in which a plunge bath was sometimes included. Swimming as a healthy exercise for all, however, was an idea that reached us in the eighties. The southern suburb of Lewisham built an establishment with first- and second-class swimming baths in 1889; other vestries followed in rapid succession. The establishments got bigger and bigger, and that of Lambeth (1897), with four swimming baths, 90 slipper baths, and provision for 64 washers, was reckoned the biggest in Europe (Fig. 59). There was some fumbling with architectural style. Lewisham's establishment was still in the démodé Gothic of the seventies; Hampstead's was "Queen Anne" in front but with a hammer beam roof over the bath. In later years, however, out of the competition jungle, a breed of specialists emerged—men like A. Hessell Tiltman and T. W. Aldwinckle—bringing the infinitely flexible "Queen Anne" to bear on the problem with the same functional elegance which had been achieved in schools.

Public baths could be made to pay. Free libraries could not, but the new literacy of the first board school generation demanded them. The vestries were reluctant and rarely moved without substantial philanthropic subsidies. Hence the Tate libraries in Lambeth. Hence also the many Passmore Edwards libraries in the remoter suburbs. The Tate fortune came from sugar, and some of it went into the building of the decidedly sugary National Gallery of British Art, otherwise the Tate Gallery, of 1897. Passmore Edwards made his money, rather surprisingly, out of architectural journalism, being proprietor of the *Building News*. Like the polytechnics and public baths, the free libraries were nearly always the subject of architectural competitions, and out of these came some exciting innovations. E. W. Mountford was as successful with libraries as he was with polytechnic institutions, and his Renaissance library at Battersea (1890) has distinction. Even more so has J. M. Brydon's in Chelsea (1890), which moves forward from "Queen Anne" right into eighteenth-century formalism (Fig. 60). The Paddington Library (1891), on the other hand, by Henry Wilson, a follower of Sedding's, is a rather wild escapade in the freest possible Gothic.

Vestry halls were another type of public building, reflecting in general the more or less disgraceful vanities of the vestrymen.

Fig. 57. Peabody Square, Islington, a typical specimen
of the housing schemes undertaken by George Peabody's
trust of 1862.

Fig. 58. The Northampton Institute, Islington (before
alteration), a product of the polytechnic movement of the
nineties. The architect was E. W. Mountford, 1893.

Fig. 59. Lambeth Public Baths, built in 1897, when it was said to be the biggest establishment of its kind in Europe.

Fig. 60. Chelsea Public Library, 1890. The architect,
J. M. Brydon, led the revival of English eighteenth-century
classicism.

Fig. 61. The British Museum of Natural History, South Kensington, 1873–81, designed by Alfred Waterhouse and faced throughout with terra-cotta.

Destined in due course to become the town halls of the London boroughs on their formation in 1899, there is not one which need detain us. Finally, the Metropolitan Board of Works built a number of unhappy-looking late Gothic fire stations before it foundered in disgrace, to be succeeded in 1889 by the London County Council. That body assembled, before the end of the century, an architectural team of the highest quality, inaugurating in its first slum clearance and rehousing project at Boundary Road (1894) the first chapter in a long and honorable twentieth-century story.

But it is time to turn to the buildings which should surely be the most representative as well as the most conspicuous elements in the image of late Victorian London—the major public buildings commissioned by the central government. What were they? Between the Houses of Parliament and the Home and India Offices in Whitehall the government commissioned very little. The latter building, where, as we have seen, Gilbert Scott and Digby Wyatt were employed in a loose partnership, was finished in 1873. In that year two major national monuments were begun: the Royal Courts of Justice, under George Edmund Street, in the Strand, and, at South Kensington, the British Museum of Natural History, under Alfred Waterhouse. Both buildings were finished around 1880, by which time they stood out, almost painfully, as mid-Victorian products in an age rapidly hardening—or softening—against such stylistic boldness as theirs. Street's early Gothic building in the Strand, as noble in scale and fastidious in detail as Westminster Abbey itself, was blamed for its archaism. Waterhouse's German Romanesque museum (Fig. 61) was more happily received; its modernity was unquestionable, but its hard, brittle, unsympathetic detail soon cast it out of favor.

It was at South Kensington, nevertheless, that Victorianism on the monumental scale really triumphed. In 1887 came the Golden Jubilee of the Queen Empress, in celebration of which a great building was recommended by the poet laureate, Tennyson. "Raise a stately memorial / Some Imperial Institute / Rich in symbol and ornament / Which may speak to the centuries." The Imperial Institute (Fig. 62) was intended to be a center for studies of the colonies and to display their resources, as well as to be a symbol of imperial glory. As an institution, it was never a total success, and it "spoke to the centuries" for only sixty years. In 1960 it was demolished, except for the tower, to make way for a college of technology in the style appropriate to such institutions.

The Imperial Institute is a memorable building. It was won in competition by Thomas Collcutt, who completed it in 1891. Standing just north of Waterhouse's museum and on the same axis, blotting out most of the Royal Horticultural Society's garden, it had the same symmetry and the same central emphasis. Stylistically, it was rooted in the Gothic revival, took something from "Queen Anne," François 1ᵉʳ, and the Quattrocento, but was still free and original, enjoying its own discipline of delicate lines, up and across, with relief ornament nicely distributed. It was perhaps *the* representative public monument of late Victorian London—not only because of its size and the sentiment it embodied, but because it so obviously issued from a tradition more concerned with domestic ease than with monumental display. It is sad that we have lost it; and the lovely tower, reset (at enormous expense) on a new base in the middle of a glass and concrete yard, is, to those who remember the building entire, nothing but a melancholy ghost.

With the Imperial Institute I must close this survey of Victorian London. Necessarily I must leave you with the impression of fearful omissions, especially because, as everybody knows, the nineties was a decade of great excitement and interest, in architecture as in the other arts. But those excitements did not much alter the architectural aspects of London till after the turn of the century and the accession of the elderly prince, who, in 1901, at long last took possession of his mother's throne. In studying the nineties it becomes inevitable to disengage what is still essentially Victorian from what one would much prefer to call Edwardian. I leave you, I hope, with a not too confused impression of what "Victorian London" may reasonably be held to mean, in the sense of an architectural panorama sixty-four years long.

Fig. 62. The Imperial Institute, South Kensington, 1887–93, designed as a celebration of Empire and demolished (except for the tower) in 1960. The architect was T. E. Collcutt.

Credits for Illustrations

Figs. 1, 2, 7, 10, 16, 19, 20, 29, 31, 33, 34, 38, 39, 41, 46, 47, 52, 53, 55, 60, 62: National Monuments Record Crown Copyright.

Figs. 3, 4, 23, 24, 27, 28, 61: Timothy Summerson.

Figs. 5, 11, 37: Royal Institute of British Architects.

Figs. 6, 8, 14, 44: J. Summerson.

Fig. 9: *London . . . exhibited in 1851* (London: John Neale, 1851), p. 749.

Fig. 12: drawn and engraved by Thos. Higham, 1838; engraving in author's collection.

Fig. 13: *Builder,* 1851, p. 739.

Fig. 15: *The Illustrated Exhibitor* (London: John Cassell, 1851), p. 28.

Fig. 17: *Illustrated London News,* Apr. 3, 1858, p. 353.

Fig. 18: Jack Skeel.

Figs. 21, 35, 40, 56: A. F. Kersting

Fig. 22: *Illustrated London News,* Feb. 25, 1860, p. 200.

Fig. 25: *Illustrated London News,* Feb. 25, 1866, p. 184.

Fig. 26: *Building News,* Mar. 20, 1869, p. 274.

Fig. 30: *Building News,* July 16, 1858, p. 723.

Fig. 32: *Building News,* Jan. 3, 1868, p. 11.

Fig. 36: James Austin.

Fig. 42: Drawing by Maurice B. Adams; *Building News,* Sept. 18, 1874; National Monuments Record Crown Copyright.

Fig. 43: *Building News,* June 25, 1875, pp. 718–19.

Fig. 45: E. R. Robson, *School Architecture* (London, 1877).

Fig. 48: *Building News,* Aug. 4, 1899, p. 145.

Fig. 49: *Building News,* July 7, 1882, p. 25.

Fig. 50: *Building News,* January 26, 1877, p. 90.

Fig. 51: *Building News,* Feb. 13, 1891, pp. 238–39.

Fig. 54: *Builder,* 1871, p. 527.

Fig. 57: *Illustrated London News,* Mar. 10, 1866, p. 233.

Fig. 58: *The Architect,* Jan. 7, 1898.

Fig. 59: *Building News,* Mar. 19, 1897, pp. 445–46.